Move over Kotter. Robin Reininger has created a new model for change that will force leaders and change consultants to take notice. In this book she does for change what Patrick Lencioni did for teams with The Five Dysfunctions. She changes the game.
Andrew Neitlich, author of *Coach!*

Be The Change uses a simple, yet very effective practice of guiding leaders through change by establishing the "events of change." They recognize that effective leadership must be able to communicate the benefits of change, as well as any impact that alters an employee's position. As a leader, Robin helps you articulate change and continually reinforce the benefits of change during the process, to alleviate the fear of the unknown and earn the trust and buy in of the rank and file.
Peter Guala, President Pathstone Advisors
Former Group President, Corporate Express

Be The Change provides leaders with a practical and actionable 6-step process for successfully dealing with change. This is far from your standard change management model. Robin masterfully uses real life events as the basis for working through change, while leveraging people first and then process to help you successfully navigate the change journey.
Vinay Kumar, PCC
Leadership Coach, Author and Speaker
Growing People * Growing Businesses

Be The Change is a must read for today's leaders faced with competing change dilemma's in their organization. Robin strategically mapped out six change events and successfully aligned the people side of the equation with the process side to help you increase the success rate of your change initiatives. Powerful book written by someone who has been a role model and a mentor/coach to me throughout my career.
Jymme McQuillan, Executive Director
Quest Diagnostics

In *Be The Change*, Robin Reininger's expertise in planning and implementation of strategic planning makes this a must-read for leaders in every organization.
> **G.B. Nanton, Editor & CEO**
> **G & H Ent., LLC**

"From decades of success leading HR in corporate America, Robin Reininger gives you a powerful lens to look at your people as the curators of your change, and guidance to leaders who need to personify positive change. *Be The Change* is that lens and guide as you step through the 6 events of change."
> **Sarah Drijfhout**
> **Founder and CEO Progeny Leadership BV**

"I wish *Be The Change* had been available decades ago. So many change models fall short when actually applied. Robin's experiences guide us in a powerful way, expertly considering all parties involved."
> **Greg Pinks, Chief Leadership Officer**
> **Axiom Performance Inc.**

Robin delivers exactly what she's experienced as a forward-thinking HR executive. Her new book, *Be The Change*, will help you with the challenges corporate executives and members of management face each day. The tools she provides along with her years of experience makes *Be The Change* a great road map for you and your company to succeed.
> **John Marino, Owner**
> **Source Recruitment Solutions, LLC**

Be the Change is an excellent resource and tool for any organization going through change. Robin Reininger takes the reader through the 6 events of change in her easy-to-follow **hr**thought Change Model. Simple, yet profoundly effective, and packed with wonderful resources. *Be the Change...* can help you navigate and guide your team forward through change.
> **Sheri Boone, MCC, Executive Coach**

be the CHANGE

A proven system to help you **command change** with confidence in your organization.

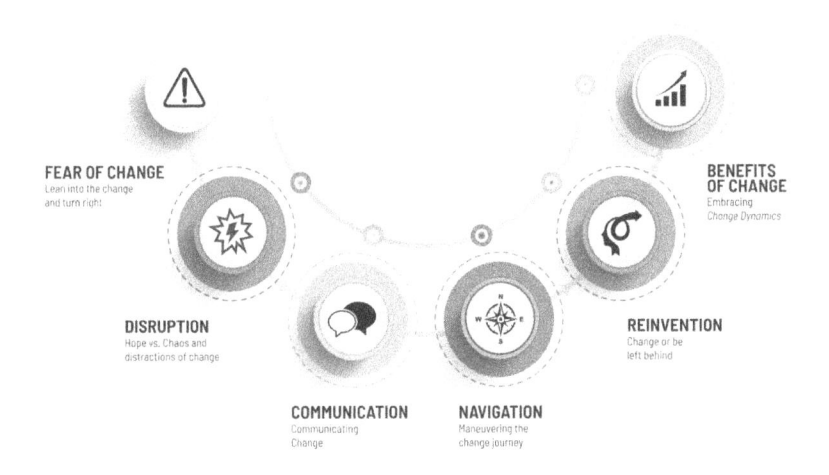

FEAR OF CHANGE
Lean into the change and turn right

DISRUPTION
Hope vs. Chaos and distractions of change

COMMUNICATION
Communicating Change

NAVIGATION
Maneuvering the change journey

REINVENTION
Change or be left behind

BENEFITS OF CHANGE
Embracing Change Dynamics

Copyright © 2019 CelebrityPress® LLC

All rights reserved. No part of this book may be used or reproduced in any manner whatsoever without prior written consent of the author, except as provided by the United States of America copyright law.

Published by CelebrityPress®, Orlando, FL.

CelebrityPress® is a registered trademark.

Printed in the United States of America.

ISBN: 978-0-9980369-1-5
LCCN: 2019930258

This publication is designed to provide accurate and authoritative information with regard to the subject matter covered. It is sold with the understanding that the publisher is not engaged in rendering legal, accounting, or other professional advice. If legal advice or other expert assistance is required, the services of a competent professional should be sought. The opinions expressed by the authors in this book are not endorsed by CelebrityPress® and are the sole responsibility of the author rendering the opinion.

Most CelebrityPress® titles are available at special quantity discounts for bulk purchases for sales promotions, premiums, fundraising, and educational use. Special versions or book excerpts can also be created to fit specific needs.

For more information, please write:
CelebrityPress®
520 N. Orlando Ave, #2
Winter Park, FL 32789
or call 1.877.261.4930

Visit us online at: www.CelebrityPressPublishing.com

be the
CHANGE

A proven system to help you **command change** with confidence in your organization.

By ROBIN REININGER

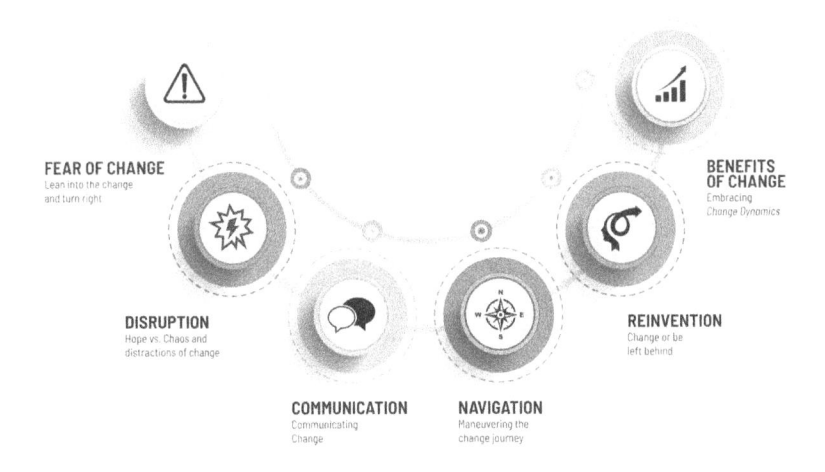

FEAR OF CHANGE
Lean into the change and turn right

DISRUPTION
Hope vs. Chaos and distractions of change

COMMUNICATION
Communicating Change

NAVIGATION
Maneuvering the change journey

REINVENTION
Change or be left behind

BENEFITS OF CHANGE
Embracing Change Dynamics

CelebrityPress®
Winter Park, Florida

DEDICATION

This book is dedicated to three very special people in my life – my mother, my son Chad, and my husband, Tom.

A special thanks to my mother who encouraged me to put forth my best effort always. Her high expectations pushed me to strive and achieve my goals and empowered me to have a positive impact on this world, and the lives of many people around me. I am grateful for the tools she gave me.

I am grateful to my son for his support and insights. Chad has been one of my biggest advocates and champions. He has also been a great thought partner. He is the one who convinced me to write *Be The Change*.

Finally, it takes a special partner to walk through life with you and accept who you are meant to be and love you all the same. I want to especially thank my husband, Tom, for always believing in me and encouraging me to pursue my dreams.

CONTENTS

Foreword 13

Preface 15

Introduction 17

Chapter 1
**INTRODUCTION OF THE hrthought
CHANGE MODEL** 19

Chapter 2
FEAR
OVERCOMING THE FEAR OF CHANGE 29

Chapter 3
DISRUPTION
THE GROUND IS SHAKING 47

Chapter 4
COMMUNICATION 63

Chapter 5
NAVIGATION
WHERE ARE WE HEADED, ANYWAY? 77

Chapter 6
REINVENTION
FROM CATERPILLAR TO BUTTERFLY 93

Chapter 7
BENEFITS OF CHANGE
A BETTER TOMORROW 113

Chapter 8
CONCLUSION
NOW IT'S YOUR TURN 135

Appendix A
Project Plan Templates 145

Appendix B
Due Diligence Activities 147

Appendix C
Summary of Coaching Questions 149

References 155

Biography 159

FOREWORD

If you have a job, you have experienced change. As humans, we tend to dislike change—we resist it just like a natural instinct. However, it does not have to be that way. In this book, you will learn how to be open to change, how you can be part of the positive "change" culture, and how you can lead others through change.

Disclaimer, the author is my mother. If I had started with that sentence, you might have overlooked the rest of the Foreword. My mother, Robin, is one of the strongest leaders I've ever met. She has been a *role model* to many throughout her distinguished career, myself included. She was my first call for help as a child, and she is still my first call today. I've sought her coaching advice, leadership expertise, and leaned on her experiences navigating change from my first job all the way through to my current position as a Software Architect.

As someone who has spent 20 years in the software industry, I have seen my share of change. Throughout my work for successful and unsuccessful software startups, well-known technology giants, and even my own software consulting business, I have seen all types of change management. The only constant is that change is guaranteed. This book shares with the reader a path through the cloudy waters that represent change. Change is a journey, often long and challenging. The time-tested and proven change model laid out in this book will teach you to lead, inspire, and listen.

Many of the lessons my mother has taught me over the years shine through in the **hr**thought Change Model. I'm proud to help her introduce *Be The Change* to you. Let her show you how to embrace change, how to avoid change for the sake of change, and how to innovate with purpose. You will come away understanding how change impacts the business, the employees and yourself.

Chad Auld

PREFACE

I was fortunate to enjoy a successful and rewarding career as a Fortune 500 Executive that taught me how to leverage change in both my professional and personal life. Therefore, I am inspired to write *Be The Change: A proven system to help you command change with confidence in your organization.*

It is with great excitement that I share with my readers a path to successfully manage through significant change events. My niche has been helping companies grow by leveraging change to develop their leaders and high-performance teams.

Change is sometimes a welcomed solution, but more often, it is unexpected and has the potential to turn your world upside down. My hope for you is that this framework for change will help you embrace the possibilities and new opportunities that change offers. *Be The Change* will guide you through effectively navigating change to achieve and/or exceed your goals.

INTRODUCTION

*The secret of **CHANGE** is to focus all of your energy, not on fighting the old, but on building the new.*
~ Socrates

Welcome to *Be The Change: A proven system to help you command change with confidence in your organization.* Changing times requires change leaders who embrace change as a journey. *Be The Change* identifies the six (6) events that occur during change in an organization and aligns the people impact and processes with each event. This model goes way beyond change management and establishes a framework to help you shift your thinking from the Fear of Change to the Benefits of Change.

Today's work environment offers many challenges, all of which have an underlying focus on people. Those challenges include:
- Leadership skill gaps
- The pace of business model changes
- Collapsing hierarchies with a focus on teams
- The increasing presence and impact of Female Leaders
- Technology Disruption
- Shifting cultures and employee demands
- Attracting, retaining, and developing talent to support the needs of the organization

Prioritizing your time as a leader and investing in the right people and types of change will make it easier to embrace the constant demands of change in the work environment today and in the future. How well you adjust to and manage change is reflective of how effective you are at connecting the people side of the equation to the change initiative process, and turning instability into opportunity. The pace of change represents a constant journey and one where you are the leader of your destiny.

Be The Change will help you effectively manage through change with a focus on connecting the people side of change to your business change initiatives so that you innovate with a purpose and leverage change as a competitive advantage. You will be introduced to the **hr**thought (pronounced hr thought) CHANGE Model that provides a framework for working through the six events of change referred to as change wheels. They are: Fear, Disruption, Communication, Navigation, Reinvention, and the Benefits of Change.

You will benefit from case studies that capture the evolution of change in organizations and share first-hand observations of when it worked well and when it did not. In addition to the case studies, *Be The Change* provides you with proven methodologies and templates to help you successfully manage through change in your organization.

CHAPTER 1

INTRODUCTION OF hrthought CHANGE MODEL

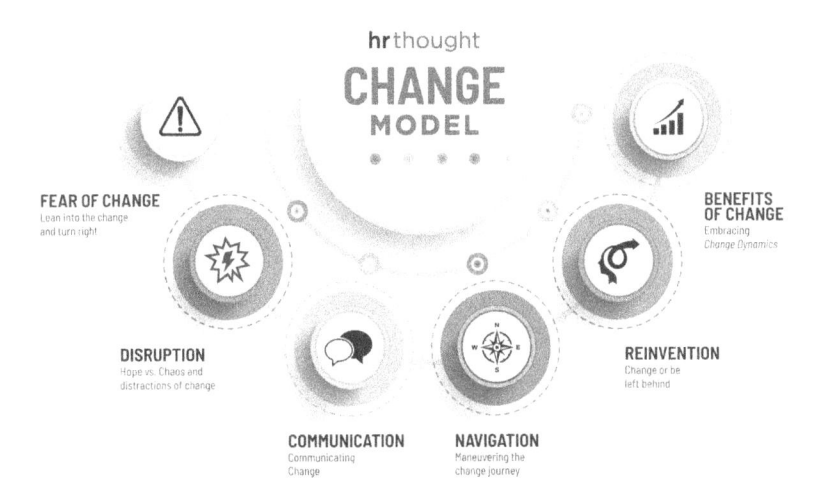

hrthought
CHANGE
MODEL

FEAR OF CHANGE
Lean into the change
and turn right

BENEFITS OF CHANGE
Embracing
Change Dynamics

DISRUPTION
Hope vs. Chaos and
distractions of change

REINVENTION
Change or be
left behind

COMMUNICATION
Communicating
Change

NAVIGATION
Maneuvering the
change journey

The **hr**thought CHANGE Model represents a practical change framework that works for organizations navigating through a large change initiative or individuals who are working through the anxiety of change. It is a model that utilizes six change wheels to guide the reader from the Fear of Change to the Benefits of Change. It is flexible and allows you to focus on one specific area where you are struggling with change, or you can follow the change dynamics as outlined in the model.

The change model diagram is visually laid out as a half circle (180 degrees) to recognize that when you reach the Benefits of Change, it takes time for people to adapt completely to the change and shift the culture. Moreover, given that up to 70% of change initiatives fail (Nohria and Beer, "Cracking the Code of Change"), it is critical to work through the change process and then continue to measure the results against the original goals.

This change model is a roadmap that provides a foundation and clarity around the inclusiveness of change and the impact on leaders, team members, and others along the way. Leaning into change with an understanding of the impact on the people side of change ensures that change efforts do not solely focus on business growth and improved profit margins and processes, only to fail later when they do not deliver the promised financial return.

Following is a preview of the six change events represented by change wheels in the model.

Change Wheel #1 – Fear of Change

This change wheel guides you through overcoming the fear of change by anticipating the impact on the business, executives, managers, individuals, and generational differences. It helps you prepare leaders for change, refocus employees to sustain productivity, walks through the initial risks and fears of change, and positions you to guide your organization through transition with a vision and purpose.

Change Wheel #2 – Disruption

Disruption is the change wheel that works through the distractions of change and helps you anticipate the disruptions from the competition. It explores the high failure rate of organizational initiatives and reviews the "watch outs" for the disruption that impacts the business and employees. This is the stage where you need to get everyone on board and have a clear endgame.

Change Wheel #3 – Communication

The third change wheel for Communication reminds us that communication is a powerful tool when navigating change. Leaders need to communicate at a level that employees can understand and carefully craft a Communication Plan that prevents unintentional messages from being delivered.

Platforms of communication are reviewed along with tips to consider when planning and executing a communication plan. Also, there is a section to help prepare you for media interaction and the impact social media can have on your organization when going through change.

Change Wheel #4 – Navigation

Navigation is the change wheel that helps you maneuver the change journey as you address the daily challenges of competitors, changing roles, direction, and survival. This includes positioning employees as ambassadors and preparing your talent for the challenges and opportunities that lie ahead.

This change wheel introduces new ways to guide the vision of change and defines the role of the manager and the coach. It also focuses on the growing importance of team effectiveness and how to make change easier for employees.

Change Wheel #5 – Reinvention

Reinvention is the transformation and transition to the new desired end state. There is a lot going on in this change wheel given the potential impact of change – new leaders, skills, systems, processes, policies, adoption, and bringing all the pieces together for a new tomorrow.

Given the pace of change today, there is an emphasis placed on reinvention that highlights the need for individuals and organizations to carefully evaluate the skills and the talent needed for the future state of the business. Reinvention is not limited to skills related to technology but the skills required for tomorrow's change leaders and the impact that collapsing hierarchies have on organizations.

Change Wheel #6 – <u>Benefits of Change</u>

Last but not least, is the Benefits of Change wheel, which focuses on a healthy work environment and the "settling in" period of change. In this stage, people start to see and believe that there is a better tomorrow and one that brings with it excitement and renewed interest around the benefits of change.

This chapter includes a list of the potential benefits of change. In addition, it also highlights the importance of a post-change analysis and provides sample templates for your convenience.

The beauty of the **hr**thought CHANGE Model is that it is timeless when it comes to managing through change. It offers a simpler way to think about and manage change, along with creating a focus on empowering your team and others to arrive at the best solution for the business and plan for managing the change journey.

FROM CORNER OFFICE TO CORPORATE COACH

You may be wondering how and why I ended up as an Executive Coach. Well, I spent most of my career, prior to founding **hr**thought, working for Fortune 500 Companies in executive positions in Human Resources and Sales.

My journey from Corporate to Coach was one of passion and the ability to share my experience and have an impact. My background spans multiple industries, including: Manufacturing, Consumer Goods, Technology, Construction, Financial Services, Professional Services, and Retail. I founded **hr**thought, LLC to

INTRODUCTION OF hrthought CHANGE MODEL

partner with companies to help grow their business by leveraging change using proven methodologies to develop leaders and high-performance teams. By understanding their biggest pain points, I help leaders find sustainable solutions to deliver business results. Now, I am the confidante who coaches executives and their leadership teams.

My passion for coaching executives and helping organizations through change initiatives comes from experiencing the pain of change firsthand as a C-suite executive. I refer to myself as a "Change Guru," given the constant change initiatives I endured. These change initiatives include acquisitions, restructuring, downsizing, and member of an executive team that executed a spin and took a company public, business model changes, union campaigns, leadership changes, and more.

As an executive, you deal with whatever comes your way. You wake up each day, and change is staring at you in the mirror. As a Certified Executive Coach, I have mastered the art of active listening and providing observations to my clients to enable them to inspire and empower their leaders and teams to successfully evaluate risk, encourage innovation, and collaborate on the best course of action for the business. Leaders who are not embracing collaboration and teams, given the collapsing hierarchy in organizations, are being left behind.

I was fortunate to have several outstanding Executive Coaches early on in my career who helped prepare me for senior level positions. The key to a great coach is finding someone you can trust, who is there in the moment for you to provide feedback and observations. An effective Executive Coach is someone who pushes you to develop new skills and builds confidence.

Coaching is not about solving problems for leaders, which tends to be the practice of many internal coaches. True coaching is about asking the right questions so that the leader can gain valuable insights. In most cases, we already know the answer! When partnered with a coach, the leader can talk through and explore the possibilities to determine what is best for the business. Trying to solve the problem for leaders ultimately leads to a lack of commitment and dissatisfaction when the plan does not work.

Most people do not like change, from the top of the organization down. Change can shake our foundations, disrupt the perfect job, require extra time and effort, create skill gaps, and cause a high level of stress. The benefits to my clients are that I lived their world and know what it takes to guide an organization through change. It takes courage, confidence, and a team to successfully navigate change.

By leveraging change through the benefit of leaders and teams, it connects people to the change equation. When leaders are prepared to manage through change, and employees understand the change and how it impacts them, they are able to navigate change more easily and embrace the Reinvention stage. With transparent goals and expectations, the communication plan proactively and almost seamlessly guides the organization through change. This, however, does not mean that some individuals will not opt out and decide the change is not right for them.

The results driven by the **hr**thought CHANGE Model include top- and bottom-line growth, efficiency savings, simplification of business processes, identification of top talent, succession planning, and leadership development. The behavior changes I have seen that deliver the most significant impact are: developing emotional intelligence (understanding yourself and others), listening, time management, building confidence, and communication skills.

My clients know that to be successful we must agree on a coaching plan that has a measurable outcome. I hold them accountable for their action plan. Recently, one of my clients told me that she knows I will hold her accountable and ask for progress updates each time we talk. She indicated that she really likes that part of the agreement because it reinforces her commitment and progress. Just the other day, she texted me to let me know that she successfully navigated a very stressful audit and attributed the outcome to the work she is doing with me. Needless to say, I was elated when I received the message!

Whether I am coaching seasoned executives, the leaders of tomorrow, or individuals starting their own business, it is gratifying to identify the behaviors that will have the biggest impact on their career and work with them to develop new skills and watch their confidence grow. Talking through the challenges and obstacles builds stronger confidence and opens up new roads of opportunities. From the micro-manager to the leader who wants to be the smartest person in the room, coaching is a way to stop limiting yourself and others based on undesirable behaviors.

CASE STUDY 1
BENEFITS OF THE hrthought CHANGE MODEL

One company, in particular, comes to mind that highlights the benefits of the **hr**thought CHANGE Model. A newly-promoted global commercial leader was charged with developing a new go-to-market strategy, along with restructuring the commercial organization in order to deliver a very aggressive target for top-line growth over the next two years.

This leader was highly regarded and had a proven track record delivering results. He had both the emotional intelligence and IQ to help him position and deliver the change. This change was no small task since there were approximately 6,000 employees in the commercial organization. And, he stepped into a role where he was managing senior leaders who had more tenure and were not necessarily happy that they did not get the job.

In my opinion, the key to his success was that he effectively worked through the Change Model with a focus on the impact on employees and alignment with the plan. He addressed the fear of change by personally meeting with each commercial leader and seeking their input. He was very influential, shared ideas, and asked for each leader's commitment. In return, he supported his leaders throughout the change process, and even took the heat from his boss a few times when things got slightly off track.

The team worked together with Human Resources to build the new model, identify risks, and develop a communication plan to communicate overall changes and individual changes to each sales consultant and assess all employees. The commercial leaders were trained on the new compensation plans and consultative selling process and had FAQ's to ensure a consistent message. The execution was amazing. They were prepared for challenges and opportunities related to individuals who had role changes and required development/coaching. Moreover, to the leader's credit, the Benefits of Change were clearly articulated with follow through on supporting all commercial employees through the change.

While this may sound easy, it took over a year from the initial planning stage to completing the training for all sales consultants to be trained on the new sales process. The benefits included a common language, standardization of compensation plans, increased profitability, top-line growth, and a stronger succession plan for the Commercial organization.

So, where do you start? What do you do first? This book will guide you through the change process as you develop new insights and confidence in your ability to manage the most difficult change initiatives.

COACHING QUESTIONS - Chapter 1

Questions to Consider When Faced With a Change Initiative:

1. What is the full scope of the change?
2. What are the possibilities and ideas behind the pending change?
3. How can I prepare my team for change?
4. Who will lead the change initiative?
5. What does the end state look like?
6. Who will be impacted by the change?
7. What external resources do I need to engage?
8. What am I missing?

CHAPTER 2

FEAR
OVERCOMING THE FEAR OF CHANGE

hr thought
CHANGE
MODEL

FEAR OF CHANGE
Lean into the change
and turn right

DISRUPTION

COMMUNICATION   NAVIGATION

REINVENTION

BENEFITS
OF CHANGE

*I've failed over and over and over again in my life,
and that is why I succeed.*
~ Michael Jordan

Change is the #1 fear in the heart of executives today. Not only does the pace of change seem faster given the disruption of technology and business models, but executives are also faced with competing change dilemmas in today's work environment and trying to figure out which change they should address first.

So why do executives fear change? To start with, the failure rate of change initiatives is so high in companies that it is difficult to manage change. According to Nohria and Beer in "Cracking the Code of Change," as high as 70% of all change initiatives fail (Nohria and Beer 2000). That failure rate can put the executive's personal reputation and career at risk. Just the sheer thought of change raises a number of concerns and fears, depending on the scale of the change. Not only is change difficult, but change requires a lot of planning, resources, and time to execute.

Depending on the experience level of the executive, they may have varying levels of comfort when it comes to managing change. Managing an anticipated rollout of a new product is one thing; executing a spin-off or major acquisition is another entirely. If the executive's style is to be involved in and approve every detail, then the success rate of the change may be decreased from the start.

Change is disruptive to organizations. Depending on the type of change and the time it takes to complete the change cycle, it distracts employees and impacts customers. There is risk to the top and bottom line results. And, typically, competitors use the distraction of change against you to convince customers that your service is not up to par, given the internal focus going on in the organization.

Needless to say, the Board of Directors will also be interested in understanding the change and impact on the business. They typically have a lot of experience and will be able to weigh in with their viewpoint and guidance. And, the executive will need to be prepared to defend their actions and address all concerns and risks, including the impact to the stock price and shareholders.

The CEO has to evaluate whether they have the right team to manage the change event. Does the team need to be developed? Where are the skill gaps? Who should lead this charge? How strong is the bench further down in the organization? What risk does the change pose to key talent? If there are skill gaps or limitations, you want to know before you get started. And, that is just the start of the questions that need to be answered.

As the planning phase evolves, the CEO will also need to think about the impact to the employee population. Will it impact a certain function, team, number of employees, or positions? In addition, what is the impact on managers and senior leaders?

Without a doubt, change is painful, its impact is felt throughout the organization, and it creates a lot of anxiety and speculation. Spending time upfront understanding what is driving the change and the advantages and downside of the proposed change is of primary importance as you think through the impact to the business. Too often leaders jump on the bandwagon of change because it is the trend and "thing to do."

Keep in mind when dealing with change that what you need is a better strategy, NOT more programs. Change and innovate with a purpose. Keep asking yourself, "What problem are we solving?" Whether you are integrating solutions, considering a massive restructuring, or implementing a new system, you need to move forward with a well-thought-out business plan that aligns people and processes. Be the Change Leader that guides with a vision and purpose with a constant eye on the implications to employees.

Below are several case studies that provide an example of change creating a negative experience and an example of change creating a positive experience.

Case Study 2
NEGATIVE CHANGE EXPERIENCE

Most employees that worked for Company A would agree that it was the best company they worked for at one point in time, and the worst company they had worked for prior to the company being acquired. The company had successfully executed hundreds of small acquisitions over the years to become one of the largest in its industry. Company A survived multiple restructuring exercises across the Regions and was really good at executing change initiatives as it acquired new companies.

While companies that were acquired were required to move to Company A's systems and expected to adopt the policies, processes, and payroll and benefit platforms, for the most part, their "mom and pop" culture was left intact. Culture was managed across the regions. Preserving the local culture of each division actually proved to be a strong suit for the company.

Company A showed top and bottom line growth over the years, had a very solid senior leadership team, and placed a strong emphasis on talent development and succession planning across the company. And, the company had what I would consider a "best in class" HR function. The project management office executed effectively, and communication was proactive and timely as a rule. Change was constant, and the joke was that if you could work for Company A, you could work anywhere.

By the end, changes were being made that did not make sense to leaders and employees, and the communication was intermittent at best. The CEO was demanding a cost of sales target that represented a significant decrease and put sales teams at risk, from the viewpoint of the field leadership. The push was to mirror the cost model of a large competitor that we were all familiar with.

As part of a major restructuring activity, Division President positions were eliminated, leaving the divisions' leaderless. There was massive confusion as the Operations and Sales Directors attempted to jointly manage the P&L with an unclear lack of accountability.

Even more frustrating to the field, the corporate office continued staffing up with MBA types creating high overhead that had to be absorbed by the field. Employees were shaking their head and trying to understand what was going on. There was limited communication, feelings of animosity in the field, and it was clear that the direction of the company had changed. Not only had it changed, but rumors were circulating that the company was being acquired.

Sure enough, nine months later, we were told that we were being acquired. Employees felt they had been sold out and that it was a big payday for the CEO. The company was acquired for its large accounts, so many of the corporate and regional employees lost their jobs during the transition.

The company had a history at one time of executing change and managing effectively through fear, disruption, communication, and navigation. However, given a change in direction, the leadership team made many confusing changes, which were poorly communicated and resulted in a lack of direction, chaos, and morale issues. This example of change highlights the contrast of how the same company that successfully executed massive changes over years of growth went sideways and failed to keep a focus on the people side of change and communication to help manage through the transition. To this day, former employees still reminisce about the good old days.

CASE STUDY 3
POSITIVE CHANGE EXPERIENCE

I still remember what I consider to be the best leadership team that I worked on in my career. I was hired into a Regional HR VP role right after Company B had gone through the largest acquisition in the history of the industry. There was a new Region President in place, and he needed a strategic HR Vice President to help him manage through duplication of resources and locations, boxes of legal issues, building a strong regional HR team, union challenges, and a host of other things on his plate. I remember him telling me flat out, "If you are transactional, I don't want you!" He was tough but fair, and he knew how to build a strong leadership team that worked together. We were the top Region for the three years that he was President.

The Region President knew what he needed to accomplish and expected everyone on the team to have a voice and to deliver. He did not favor one member or functional area over another since he needed each one of us to execute on the goals in our area. All division leaders had to apply for their positions after the acquisition, and the most qualified leaders were selected to run the divisions. Facilities had to be shut down, cessation contracts negotiated, consistent processes and policies had to be rolled out, succession plans implemented, business reviews were standardized and mandatory for us to sit through, and there were systems and multiple challenges to deal with every day.

Given the volume and scope of work to be done, people were working a lot of hours to hit deadlines. There was a significant amount of travel to juggle, as well. The Region President had high expectations but also trusted and empowered his team to manage the change. He scheduled weekly updates with the entire team. The team was cohesive and looked out for one another. If we saw something that our counterpart(s) needed to know, we were expected to communicate and follow up.

That experience stretched each member of the team and also reinforced the power and benefits of change. We addressed each change wheel as a team. We were prepared and supported to manage through fear, disruption, communication, navigation, and reinvention. We clearly understood what the end state looked like and had a focus on getting the right people in the right job.

As a team, we were a resource for the Divisions and capitalized on teaching moments to share best practices and guide the organization through change immersion. The pace was fast and the expectations high, but knowing that we had the support of the

Division President, we pushed forward every day to ensure that we delivered on our commitments.

This experience was not only positive but it prepared me for future roles as I climbed the Corporate Ladder.

IMPACT ON THE BUSINESS

When contemplating a change for the business, one of the first things that an executive needs to evaluate is what is driving the change. The worst thing to do is to change for the sake of change or because it appears to be a trend in the market/industry. Trends come and go, and change requires carefully thinking through how a change will impact the employees and the business.

You need to develop a comprehensive change strategy if the decision is to move forward. An insightful coach once told me to make sure that I carved out quality time to think through strategy because I was good at it. It is good advice to remember to schedule that "quality thinking" time when you get caught up in the change cycle.

There are many types of change that can impact a business. These changes can come in many forms and be large or small change initiatives. Examples of common changes in companies are acquisition, spin, restructuring, change of leadership, change of ownership, shutdown, culture shift, business model change, name change, and new system implementations. The nature of the change will dictate who needs to be involved in and leads the change process.

For instance, in the case of an acquisition, the senior leadership team, Finance, Human Resources, IT, Operations, and Legal will be asked to weigh in on the due diligence process and help identify the milestones/activities that need to be incorporated into the project plan for each respective area. Staffing the acquisition team with functional experts who understand and will be impacted by the change helps to lessen fear and the failure rate and ensure key steps are not missed.

As you build the change strategy and project plan, it is equally important to agree on how you will measure the success of the change. You will need to create a baseline of where you are today, and then measure against your results when the change is complete. For instance, the rationale behind change could be to decrease operating expenses by restructuring the Operations function, including closing unprofitable facilities, eliminating a level of management, and automating several key processes.

Assuming the above scenario of decreasing operating expenses, let's work through what this might look like if you were told to reduce operating expenses by $40M as a result of a restructuring initiative. As part of the restructuring, you plan to close unprofitable facilities, eliminate a layer of management in Operations, and work with IT to automate several inventory-tracking processes.

For each of these goals, you must identify the baseline cost prior to the change and set goals/metrics to measure against when the restructuring is completed. Your current operating expenses are $600M. So reducing expenses by $40M will make your new operating expenses or goal $560M.

When the restructuring activity is complete, you achieve a savings of $20M from closing ten underperforming facilities, a savings of $10M based on eliminating ten Regional Operations positions, and the automation of inventory processes is expected to generate a $7M savings. Your total savings is $37M, which falls short of the $40M goal. You missed your target by $3M and will need to explain to the Senior VP of Operations why you missed the goal and how you will make up the shortfall.

You will find sample project plan templates in Appendix A that you can use to document the goals and metrics for your future change initiatives. The process starts with a high-level corporate project plan detailing the specific goals and metrics. Each functional area would have a project plan with their specific goals and metrics to roll up to the corporate plan to ensure alignment of milestones, goals, metrics, ownership, and resources.

Once the plan is complete, the CEO may need to communicate the proposed changes to the Board. They will provide them with an overview and analysis of the plan to get their approval. They will also need to identify the functional areas and individuals who need to be involved based on the change, and the due diligence required by each function. See Appendix B, Due Diligence Activities, for further information on critical items to include in your due diligence evaluation.

Change can be a significant undertaking. So, when the Fear of Change wheel tells you to "lean in and turn right," it means you have to embrace the change and plan for the appropriate actions, taking into consideration the impact on people and the business. And, you will be asking employees to accept change and make changes that they do not want to make.

BE A CHANGE MAKER

When you accepted your role as an executive, you probably assumed that your primary responsibilities were to lead a group of people and make decisions. I guess they forgot to tell you that you signed up to be a Change Maker. Your job is to lead the way and come up with a Master Plan for Change. Your primary role will ultimately become managing the expectations, communication, and requests from the Board.

My first piece of advice to you is to be authentic and as transparent as you can. There is nothing worse than losing the trust of the organization. Employees are looking to you for guidance and honesty. And, how well you lead the organization through change and manage your stress level will undoubtedly have an impact on your legacy and how you are viewed as a leader. As a suggestion, start by viewing change as a learning experience and evaluate the opportunities/risks as a result of change.

Your executive presence, personal style, and influence in the organization can be an asset to you during change. Be approachable, listen, create a collaborative environment, and focus on team effectiveness to prepare the organization for change. Employees will look to you as their leader and watch how you handle change and listen to how you communicate the news about change.

Your challenge is to balance the strategic, tactical, and people impact of the change and to identify the key resources and overarching plan to get you there. What's the worst thing that can happen? You fail. It is perfectly reasonable to be afraid or nervous in times of change, but you can do this! Your job is to be the change leader and to help manage others up during the change.

It is absolutely crucial that your leadership presence is felt in the organization during times of change. But, the good news is that you have a team and you do not have to manage all the details of the change by yourself. However, you will need to quickly understand the strengths of your team and areas where they need to be developed. You need a high-performance team.

This is an excellent time to think about an Executive Coach for you and your team. An Executive Coach can work with team members to provide a clear understanding of strengths, limitations, leadership attributes, and development needs. The Coach will prepare a personal development plan reflecting clear expectations and help each employee explore insights and possibilities in a safe environment.

Executive coaching is a way to help individuals work through difficult decisions, challenges, or behavior changes to create sustainable change solutions. Outcomes may include: improving financial performance, accelerating change, improving the success rate of new leaders, and improving productivity.

A functional area that is often neglected when it comes to talent development is Human Resources. This team supports leadership development for key employees, but often an investment is not made in senior HR leaders to prepare them for change and supporting the organization's needs. As a suggestion, having a Coach for the head of Human Resources is a gift to the individual and recognition of the importance of the role. Making this investment can pay off huge dividends.

The timing of the communication about the change is also critical so that you are as transparent about the change as possible and get ahead of the rumors. Once the rumors start, you can expect to see the beginning of disruption to the business. Employees will be speculating about the change. Every time there is a closed-door meeting or a visitor shows up, employees will be talking amongst themselves and sharing their opinions and those of others who "saw what happened." It is human nature to attempt to make sense out of ambiguity and the unknown, but it is the responsibility of leadership to keep the rumor mill from creating a toxic work environment.

Getting everyone on board the change train is hard. You will have early adopters and late adopters. But, you need to be clear to everyone that when the "train leaves the station" that the change journey has begun, and there is no turning back. And, in some cases, individuals will make a personal choice along the journey to move on rather than face the change.

The faster you develop and agree on a comprehensive plan of action, communicate the plan, and refocus the organization, the less disruption to your business. A big key to your success is to start with understanding the impact on people, and coach your leaders on how to manage through change. The impact on people means that you need to have a diverse team that helps to develop and manage the change strategy. Diversity offers you critical perspectives that will be missed if you elect to only solicit feedback and ideas from the leadership team.

Change impacts both your professional and personal life as an executive. You must find a way to alleviate the stress with a goal of work-life "blend." That means keeping your priorities in order and balancing your role as an executive with competing priorities in your life.

I remember my husband asking me at one point, when I was working on a spin-off, when he was going to be a priority. That is eye-opening! So, set the example to your team and respect their personal lives.

At the end of this chapter are some suggested questions to help you plan for change. For now, let's explore the impact on your Managers.

IMPACT ON MANAGERS

It is important to recognize that your Managers—and especially the front-line supervisors—experience the biggest impact of the change since they have to manage their day-to-day responsibilities and also implement and manage all change initiatives. And, unfortunately, they are not privy to the high-level conversations and strategy sessions that take place. So, often they are faced with implementing a change in which they had little to no input and do not fully understand the why and how of the equation.

Managers are looking for direction from the organization during a change event. That direction is more than a quick meeting with FAQs. Managers feel the stress of the change because they do not always have the answers to employee questions. So, they feel unprepared and isolated. But, at the end of the day, the Managers are the ones to whom the employees will go to when they seek advice and updates. The Manager is the one the employee relates to, and in many cases, the reason they work for and stay with the company. So, if Managers are not prepared, you risk losing talent.

Do not assume that your managers are prepared for or experienced in managing change. Depending on their tenure, time in the position, or management experience, their ability to manage change will vary significantly. Thus, their perspective of managing through change will be different than executives. In addition, do not assume that their manager will sufficiently train them or communicate to them throughout the change process. I cannot count the number of times that managers told me that they never received an important communication that was to be communicated downward from their boss.

It is best to assume that communication is not always cascaded down through the organization through managers. You will need to establish a method to communicate directly to managers and employees. Are your managers experienced and are they trained in change management? If not, what training do they need? Do you have an internal resource to conduct the training, or is it better to hire an external resource or consultant?

How do you ensure that your Managers have a support network? Who will they go to when they have questions and concerns? And, keep in mind, that they may resist change if they don't fully understand the reason behind the change and the direction the company is going. Change disrupts people's routine and careers, so this is a group where your time is well spent getting them on board and preparing them to manage change.

A perfect example that comes to mind is when we were rolling out a new bonus communication to managers in a company where I worked. The previous process was driven more from a Human Resources perspective. But, it obviously made more sense for the employee to hear from their manager regarding how the bonus was calculated, how personal objectives were factored in, and the final bonus award. The manager made the recommendations and was instrumental in the approval process. If it came from Human Resources, and the employee had questions beyond how it was calculated, they were not in an ideal position to answer. Despite preparing and training the managers on the communication and stressing the importance of the conversation with the employee, there were about 50 employees who did not have a conversation with their manager but had a bonus or no bonus show up in their paycheck.

Who are the critical players? Do you have a succession plan in the event a manager leaves? Will the change impact some of these positions? Are retention bonuses needed to get through the change? Too many times, senior leaders expect managers to do as they are told. This may not be the time to take that risk. The more communication and time spent working with this group, the higher the success rate to execute the change across the company.

IMPACT ON INDIVIDUALS

The biggest concern for most individual employees is, "How does this impact me?" Does it impact my job? Does it require retraining? Will I still get paid on the same day? Will I still have benefits? Are there new opportunities? How do I apply for new positions? These are just some of the questions for employees during times of change.

Even though most individuals do not like change, change is a common occurrence in the workplace. That does not mean that change does not create anxiety and make people uncomfortable. In fact, for those individuals who have never been through change in the workplace, they are afraid and do not know what to expect.

There will be early adopters of change, late adopters, and some that fall in the middle. Some employees will see change as yet "another adventure or another change," while other employees will be afraid of the unknown, instability, and start speculating on the reason for change and who will be impacted.

I remember receiving a call several years ago from my son one day when he was at work. He was whispering on the phone, and he said, "Mom, people are going in and out of the conference room and not coming back to their desk. Something is going on. I think some of my friends were let go." We laugh about it now, but at the time, he was a recent college grad working for a large company away from home. He had never been through a restructuring event, and it was frightening. I knew he was shaken and afraid they were going to call his name next. So, I told him to keep working, and that I was sure there would be a communication to the employees once it was over. He texted me at the end of the day that it was over, he was safe, and that "X" number of employees were let go due to the business results in the last quarter.

Change impacts all employees when friends and co-workers leave the organization. Never underestimate the impact change has on less tenured and newly-hired employees. They may be shaking in their shoes! I strongly suggest that each manager communicate with their team immediately following an event that results in the loss of jobs. It is essential to communicate the change and to understand their concerns. The other challenge is that the remaining employees may have to pick up the additional workload. This, justifiably, can cause further morale issues. Keep in mind that you should plan to work with your Human Resources and Communication Departments to deliver consistent messaging.

Training and communication that matter to this group of employees are important, just like with the managers. The message needs to be geared toward individual employees with an understanding of how they will be impacted and addressing those issues that are relevant or important to them.

It is advisable to conduct the communication and training at a local level and in person. That can be accomplished by having the manager, a senior manager/leader present, and a Human Resources representative. This promotes consistency, support from the top of the organization down, and provides several subject matters to answer all of their questions.

As you can see, the potential impact to the business and employees can be staggering if you do not develop a plan that connects the people side of the equation to the change initiative. In summary, you will be well served to put the time and effort into training your leaders, building a change plan, and communicating throughout the change process.

COACHING QUESTIONS - Chapter 2

Below are some suggested Coaching Questions you may want to consider when planning for change:

1. Who do you need to engage first?
2. How prepared is your team to manage change?
3. What are the skill gaps?
4. Which team members need to be involved immediately?
5. What concerns will the Board of Directors raise?
6. Who can you trust?
7. How much information do you need to share and how deep in the organization?
8. How will the change impact your financial targets for the year?
9. What are the trade-offs?
10. Who can lead the change effort?
11. Do you need a PMO (project management office)?
12. Who will head the PMO?
13. What does an ideal project plan look like to manage the change?
14. What are the key milestones that need to be addressed?
15. How and when will you communicate the change?
16. How do you address fears and rumors?
17. Who will the change impact from an organizational standpoint?
18. What are your options?
19. What are the risks?
20. How will the change impact your customers?
21. How will you handle the competition?
22. What can go wrong?
23. Who are the hi-potential talent risks?
24. Will you need retention bonuses?

CHAPTER 3

DISRUPTION
THE GROUND IS SHAKING

hrthought
CHANGE
MODEL

FEAR OF CHANGE

BENEFITS OF CHANGE

DISRUPTION
Hope vs. Chaos and distractions of change

REINVENTION

COMMUNICATION   NAVIGATION

Innovation distinguishes between a leader and a follower
~ Steve Jobs

CHANGE IS THE ONLY CONSTANT

How many times in your career have you been told that change is the only constant? Some wise person you worked with probably offered you this advice when the company you were working for announced a new change initiative. In other words, "change" really means that you can expect to continually navigate change in your professional and personal life. Change challenges the status quo, helps you grow as an individual and brings with it varying degrees of disruption.

The first time I heard the term "disruption" as it related to a business change, was when I was sitting in a meeting with a new CEO. He was referring to disrupting the industry with a new business model that would dramatically increase the speed to market for our customers. Leaders set out to make a difference, and it was apparent that we had a new leader who was going to change the world.

I quickly learned that innovation could be disruptive. We can certainly debate the meaning of disruption and the impact it has across markets, industries, and consumers. However, according to John Hagel, "True disruption unseats the leading incumbents in a particular market or industry." (Hagel 2016). One thing is clear to me. When I worked in organizations where there were "disruptions," there was a strong leader at the top of the organization, and "the ground was shaking." In other words, change was happening and being led from the top of the organization.

It is a given that change is unavoidable and a constant challenge for executives today. In fact, many executives tend to be overwhelmed by the disruption of change. But, most of us would agree that if you are not experiencing change in your company, you are not growing and leading the way in your market space. Disruption and innovation are clearly change-drivers.

There are a number of studies on the failure rate of organizational initiatives. Those studies estimate failure rates to be anywhere from 60%-70%. And, the primary cause of failure is due to the leader's inability to implement change due to their managerial capacity being underdeveloped (Ashkenas 2013). Yet **53%** of employees surveyed report no leadership development opportunities in their organization (Lavoie 2017).

In order to understand how to drive change and disruption, let's think about some of the disruptions we face in today's business environment. The first thing that comes to mind is digital disruption, which ranges from big data to social media. As my son explained it to me, big data is taking massive amounts of data and sorting and managing it via reporting and spreadsheets so the information can be analyzed. Social media has also forever disrupted the way we communicate with each other. Instead of previous methods of communication like phone calls or letter writing, we go to Facebook and LinkedIn to find out what our friends and colleagues are doing and share our own personal and professional information for others to see and interact with.

Disruption can also include business model changes, supply chain solutions, new products, technology, driverless cars, and the multi-channel workforce we are experiencing today. Disruption impacts both the business and its employees. And, disruption is clearly a part of the business cycle that is famous for creating chaos and confusion. When disruption hits an organization, many employees will find themselves in survival mode.

Employees will ask a lot of questions, depending on the type of disruption to the organization. Who is in charge? Who can you trust? What does this mean for me? Do I leave or stay? What is the end game? What is the real reason behind the change? So, be prepared to field the questions.

CASE STUDY 4
HOSTILE TAKEOVER

This case study is about Company B that went through a hostile and unexpected takeover. It shook the foundation of the company and was met with animosity by senior leaders.

I remember the day the call came in for the President, and he was not in the office. His executive assistant attempted to connect the CEO of the company spearheading the takeover to one of our senior leaders that the CEO knew in our company. But, believe it or not, the Senior VP would not take the call! Needless to say, this was just the start of major disruption and change to the business over the next year.

There was a lot of shouting that went on when the President returned to the office and connected with his boss. Shortly thereafter, the President was out of a job. And, four of his senior leaders chose to leave immediately with him.

There was a lot of fear in the organization as to what this meant for the remaining employees. There were interim assignments made to cover the open positions, and new faces flew in and out with a lot of meetings behind closed doors.

It was the most uncomfortable environment I have ever worked in during my career. You did not know what was happening from day to day. There were individuals jockeying for positions. And, you felt that you could not trust anyone. Employees were distracted. There was a lot of whispering on the phone. You could practically hear a pin drop on the carpet – it was so quiet.

Finally, a new President was named and came on board. He put his new team in place, shared his vision, and spent time getting to know employees and incorporating some of their ideas.

Things settled down over time, and there were actually more career opportunities and better benefits as a result of the takeover. In addition, the company now had a national footprint and expanded its product line to be able to market to high-end consumers and capitalized on supply chain efficiencies. The company was well positioned for, and experienced significant growth over the next few years, to become one of the largest in its industry.

I would attribute the success of Company B to strong leadership, a clear vision, and timing in the market. It was well managed, had innovative designs, and the senior leadership team understood how to motivate and reward employees.

DISRUPTIVE LEADERSHIP

There is "disruption" and then there are "disruptive leaders." Disruptive leaders are laser-focused on a vision, purpose, and possibilities. They see the big way out-of-the-box picture and embrace change and disruption with a passion that is hard to match. For them, disruption is an exciting adventure that has no fear or boundaries.

The one true disruptive leader that I worked with in my career worked day and night. He was brilliant, but had total disregard for people's personal lives. It was terrific to work with this CEO and witness how his mind worked. He was over-the-top competitive, talked at a level that people struggled to comprehend, and never stopped. Unfortunately, he assumed and expected that everyone was as enthusiastic about the future and his ideas as he was.

We started financial reviews at 6 am in the morning at my location, but based on time zone differences, there were colleagues at their computers at 4 am in the morning and often sitting on calls at midnight or 1 am on a regular basis. You could argue that is part of doing business in a global organization. The CEO got involved in everything and he was known for last-minute presentation changes and blowing up projects and starting over. And, that took a toll on the people that worked for and with him.

But, the thing that really got employees' attention was when one of the senior leaders could not go on vacation with his family because a strategic plan had to be redone. The senior leader wanted to leave for a short time and take his family to the airport to say goodbye. But, he was told to get a car service because the CEO did not want to interrupt the planning process. So much for family being a priority!

Disruption can be consuming and confusing. Throughout the change process, it serves the executive well to listen, remain objective, tune in to possibilities, acknowledge limiting beliefs, and balance short-term and long-term gains related to the disruption. Disruptive leaders would be wise to negate disruptive behaviors exhibited by themselves and others. Allowing disruptive behaviors and internal politics to prevail within the organization is dangerous and can be damaging to the reputation of the executive and the company.

The scale of disruption can be small or large, depending on the magnitude of the change. There are both positive and negative impacts that play out during disruption, and great leaders know how to capitalize on the positives that others may not have considered.

Table 1. Positive versus Negative Impact of Disruption

Positive Impact of Disruption	Negative Impact of Disruption
Helps identify future leaders	Creates fear
Develops skills and talent	Loss of jobs
Raises the bar	Automation of jobs
Move ahead of the competition	Causes confusion
Erases the status quo and old ideas	Anger/denial
Focuses on new possibilities	Creates chaos and sometimes crisis
Better end game for customers	Damages a company's reputation if it fails
Resets boundaries	Internal politics can get in the way
Growth	Loss of productivity, revenue, or profit during change
Transformation of industry	Plan not executable

Despite the resistance to change, the disruptive leader will push forward using their influence to convince others that leaving their big idea on the table would be a huge mistake. Many disruptive leaders do not seem to have the patience for handling all the details behind the plan. But, in the previous example that I referenced, the CEO was outstanding and could be talking about vision at 9,000 feet and come down to 500 feet and work through the details.

The lieutenants surrounding the disruptive leader need to be strong enough and have the courage to push back when there is risk to the plan, not enough resources, or unexpected challenges along the way. The effectiveness of the lieutenant can also be reflective of their relationship with the leader, respect or need for the value they add, or the temperament and personality of the leader.

The executives who lead change/disruption in their business, versus being considered a disruptive leader, typically have different attributes. They may be focused on a reorganization change within the company, cost-cutting, operational efficiencies, acquisition, or change in leadership. This leader is typically more focused on planning, financial impact, and change management versus the big out-of-the-box ideas or a major disruption that changes the industry. Regardless of the type of change, change creates a level of disruption to the business.

These examples are not intended to stereotype leaders but to gain insights into the styles and behaviors that drive a disruptive leader versus a leader who is managing through change/disruption in their organization. Table 2 explores some of the differences between the two types of leaders:

Table 2. Disruptive Leader vs. Leader Managing Change/ Disruption in the Business

Disruptive Leader	Leader Managing Change/ Disruption
Entrepreneurial	Strong Business Acumen
Super smart – High IQ	Intelligent – could have High IQ
Vision of Possibilities	Strategic Vision
Change Maker	Change Leader
Relentless	Driven
Focused on Funding Ideas	Budget Focused
Innovative – Break Conventions	Innovative
Risk Taker/Fearless	Calculated Risk Taker
Looking for the Next Big Thing	Looking for Next Steps
Make it up as They Go – Unstructured	Plan and Analyze – Structured
Expectations of Others Beyond Reality	High Expectations
Almost Zero Work-Life Blend	Limited Work-Life Blend
Chaotic Work Environments	Organized Chaos
Break-neck Speed	Timelines and Resources Drive Speed
Personal Ambitions #1 Priority	Ambitious but Accountable for Delivering Goals

The disruptive leader is focused on beating the competition to market, especially in the case of technological advances. They often have a vision beyond reality, big money from investors, and have to move at a crazy speed before someone disrupts ahead of them. I have seen these leaders charting new territory and making up the rules as they go. In the process, they often create a chaotic whirlwind as they continuously change direction and make promises to others along the way. They have a tendency to take ideas 80% of the way to completion and then hand it off and chase the next big thing or change course and go in another direction. The downside of this is that crucial pieces of information were sometimes missed in the process.

These leaders are very talented, but given the pace and magnitude of some of the disruptions, they can also display disruptive behavior. An excellent example of this for me was Steve Jobs when he founded Apple and was ousted from the CEO role during his first tenure with the company. When he came back, he seemed to take a different approach and more consciously balanced the people side with the business. He was still a disruptive leader driven by success, but he appeared to have learned from his earlier behavior/approach and displayed more control and stronger leadership skills.

My son works in tech. His first few jobs in Silicon Valley after college ranged from big names to scrappy start-ups. He experienced disruption first-hand, but also worked for several disruptive leaders.

I gained some valuable insights from my son through his experience. For starters, he reminded me that approximately 90% of startups fail, so the pressure is tremendous in a startup work environment. He also said it is not just about being part of a team working on disruptive products, but it includes disruptive experiences that impact marketing, technology, and cultures. He recalled working on a project for five months with the support and approval of the CEO, only to have it scrapped and told to switch to a different technology.

So, despite working long hours and weekends and putting a strain on your personal life, these kinds of jobs ultimately create burnout for their employees and an unhealthy and unsustainable lifestyle. Employees find themselves feeling demotivated based on the time and effort they put in without recognition for the great work they actually contribute.

Like all forms of change in a business, the employees will experience stress, longer hours, heavier workloads, and high expectations, regardless of the leader's style. Most leaders are ambitious, focused on results, and working through daily challenges. While change is hard and requires people to adapt, the leader's ability to engage and motivate while balancing the challenge will likely produce better results from employees.

The callout to leaders is to have a plan to effectively manage through change and to plan and manage the impact on their employees. When employees are connected to the change and understand how they are personally impacted as well as how their role contributes to the overall goals, the success rate of retaining talent increases.

HOPE vs. CHAOS: THE DISTRACTIONS OF CHANGE

The distractions of change are often underestimated when it comes to the impact on employees. The impact of change also has a correlation to the scale of change being experienced by the organization and the employees.

There are many things to keep an eye out for when it comes to managing the stress level of change in the workplace. The first starts with how the change is communicated to the organization. The more clarity and transparency around the change event, the more likely the employees will understand what is happening. If employees are presented with a vague description of the change and timeline, there is a higher likelihood that they will speculate and share their perspectives with other employees.

The second warning sign to watch out for is the relationship employees have with their manager, and if they trust their manager to tell them the truth. When engagement surveys are conducted, this is a key question that provides a lot of insight into how management is viewed from the top down. When organization changes are announced and managers are impacted, this is another distraction. It can cause distrust for employees to be worried about their own job and anticipate change in the organization. The way you communicate these types of changes and make the transition is another critical milestone.

Keep in mind that any kind of change in the workplace tends to make employees feel less secure. So, getting employee buy-in is a way to lessen the negative impact of change on the business. When people lose control or their routine faces uncertainty, their stress level increases. Workplace stress, if not carefully managed can often result in employees calling off work and taking unexpected leaves of absence, including filing workers compensation claims.

Employee morale can deteriorate during change. When jobs are eliminated, friends and co-workers are impacted, new skills are required, or there are new policies and procedures rolled out, employee engagement may drop. This most often results in lower productivity rates from employees. I do not need to tell you that lower productivity impacts business results. Distracted employees may also start rumors based on their speculation of what is really going on. That distraction could also mean higher injury rates.

When an employee has to learn a new job, is faced with learning new technology, or a new reporting method, management should keep in mind that everyone learns at a different pace and in a different way. So, you need to think about how to deploy training using multiple methodologies, including: visually, written instructions, hands-on, or simulated training.

And, finally, politics can factor into organizations during times of change. It may be hard to believe, but there are always people jockeying for positions or trying to be an exception to the new rules. Exceptions to the rules insert doubt and chaos. Ultimately politics and ulterior motives mean leadership cannot enforce the rules.

I worked for several large companies where the Sales VP pushed for a change in sales compensation and also stood behind the program when it was rolled out. In both cases, the program was well thought out and well communicated to the sales force. The programs were designed to increase sales and profitability, and they did. And, where there was a new compensation system, there was a deadline set for all sales reps to be on the system and in compliance. But, I also worked in one organization where leadership was afraid to standardize/change the compensation plan and enforce the changes. No one said that change was easy.

A great example of politics in an organization is when a new sales compensation program is rolled out. Sales management may try to make exceptions for special sales reps. I have even seen sales managers try to create a separate program for their top sales rep so that the rules do not apply. Time and time again, when a compensation analysis is performed for the sales force, the top selling reps do not produce the highest margins or margin dollars. So, when it comes to politics, the senior leader needs to be prepared to stand firm and deal with the conflict that is likely to occur.

Employees will search for hope vs. chaos during change in the business. Their hope comes in many forms:

- Surviving the change
- Being able to hold up under the stress level
- Adapting to the new changes
- Mastering new skills
- Navigating the politics
- Finding an exit strategy.

WHAT'S THE END GAME?

So, what is the "End Game?" Does it mean you successfully completed the change process? Is the organization finished with all the changes? Can employees get back to normal? What is the new normal? Most importantly, "Is it a better place?"

The **hr**thought CHANGE Model suggests there is a new kind of change management to help you manage through change. The model is designed to focus on major change events that occur throughout the change process. It then connects the people impact and planning process for a winning combination to help you successfully achieve your goals. It places emphasis on identifying the events that need to be addressed during change, focusing on the impact on people, and aligning the processes and plan.

As a leader, you need to "Be the Change" that makes a difference in leading the organization through change dynamics. It takes discipline and courage to tackle change and deal with adversity along the way. It is important to remember that true leadership is about doing the right thing. It may feel uncomfortable, and in fact, you may experience unpopular reactions. And, regardless, there is always a cost to change.

The end game is really about what you set out to achieve when you started. But, until all the pieces are in place, you do not reach the end game. Change is exhausting for everyone. And, just because you reached a major milestone does not mean that the work is done.

An example that comes to mind for me is when I was part of a senior leadership team tasked with spinning off a business unit and taking it public. The parent company had a solid strategy with a project plan to guide us through the critical milestones for each functional area. But, when we stood together on the platform at the Stock Exchange, and the CEO rang the bell, the work was far from over.

To reach the end game, there were still systems that had to be fully implemented, work-a-rounds that had to be automated, programs to be integrated, leadership teams to be aligned, talent that was in transition, and an analysis of what worked and did not work. And, there was always the question of, "What's next?"

There is a cost to change, as we have discussed throughout this book. That cost can be financial rewards to the executive team for achieving the goals, the loss of key talent, the transition of new talent, failure to achieve the targeted savings and synergies, morale issues in the new organization, failure to fully embrace change opportunities and retain the status quo, loss of employee benefits, or new benefits for employees. Whatever the cost, you cannot make everyone happy, and the organization typically suffers some degree of setback.

At the end of every change, it is important to understand what worked and what did not work. There will be varying opinions, silent losses, and a renewed focus on the future. At some point, employees will welcome an opportunity to move forward and embrace the new normal. As the organization works to institutionalize the changes into the culture, leaders must recognize that it takes time to shift the culture.

Too often, the organization is off and running again before the dust settles from the previous change event. It is no wonder that initiatives fail primarily based on management capability. Organizations do not allow enough time to complete the change cycle prior to starting the next big thing.

So, what is the end game and when does it end? Perhaps it ends with the lifecycle of one executive and the beginning of new leadership with the next executive.

COACHING QUESTIONS - Chapter 3

Below are some suggested Coaching Questions to consider when working through "Disruption":

1. What is the purpose behind the disruption?
2. What are the risks?
3. What can be done to minimize the disruption to the employees and the business?
4. How does disruption help us move ahead of the competition?
5. How will the competition react?
6. What does disruption mean to our customers?
7. What is the expected timeframe for the disruption?
8. Are we at risk of losing key talent?
9. What are we missing?
10. What is the message to the sales force?
11. What tools do we need for the sales force?
12. What politics are being played in the organization?
13. What is the "End Game?"

CHAPTER 4

COMMUNICATION

People don't resist change. They resist being changed.
~ Peter Senge

SPEAKING SO THEY LISTEN

Communicating change requires a strategy and a communication plan to enable you to effectively communicate. This stage of change requires a lot of planning and involvement from senior leaders because it ultimately defines how you "talk about change to the organization." Speaking so they listen means you need to communicate a purpose and articulate the change with words that your employees understand. Too often, I have seen leaders communicate at a level that the average employee does not understand.

An excellent starting point in the communication process is to define the purpose:

- What is the change?
- How will it impact the business?
- How will it impact the employees?
- What can employees expect, and when?

Do not underestimate the power and influence of communication. It is best to be open and honest with employees. Keep the communication simple and to the point. Tell them as much as you can or know. Make it personal so that they feel you are speaking to them and not at them.

An easy way to remember how to effectively communicate is **PACC**. It stands for:

P – Purpose
A – Audience
C – Clear
C – Concise

What is the purpose of your communication? Who is your audience? Is your message clear so that everyone understands what is happening? And, is your communication concise and to the point?

As you build your communication plan, you need to decide who should be involved in the planning process, in addition to senior leadership. Obviously, depending on the scale of the change, you may need to consult with external resources. Do you have a Communication Department that can manage this process? Who will be the executive sponsor? Who will represent Legal, HR, Investor Relations, and other departments that need to be involved? How and when do you involve the Board of Directors or get their approval?

Change initiatives often create a new vocabulary of words for the organization that will be adopted and understood over time. For instance, if an organization goes through a restructuring exercise, some of the terms that may be used are: restructuring, WARN notice, severance package, and retention bonus. While they seem fairly straightforward to many of us, do not assume that all employees understand the terms. Does a restructuring mean a one-time event where a department or region is impacted? Or does it mean that leaders will be impacted? What is the severance package? Who is eligible for a retention bonus? You get what I mean. Clarity is important to help balance the message.

There are a number of other things to think about during a potential change. How will this impact the culture of the organization? What are the inconveniences and opportunities that change represents? How will the managers take the news? How do you prepare the managers for change? What mediums will you use to communicate change? What habits will you be breaking? What new ideas are you introducing to the organization? There is so much to think about and plan for when it comes to change.

CASE STUDY 5
EFFECTIVELY EXECUTING CHANGE

There is one company that I worked for that excelled in the planning, communication, and execution of change initiatives.

Company D is a well-established Fortune 500 company that had a change in leadership several years ago. Along with that change of leadership came other leadership changes in the business units. Change is a common event in this organization. But, Company D differentiates itself by placing a focus on people, leadership, and teams and actually living the organizational values. Those values are well publicized and communicated across the globe to all employees and customers.

As a worldwide leader in the industry and a company that has won multiple awards for technology and sustainability, Company D understands the importance of its reputation when it comes to employer and employee branding. And, whether the company is facing a restructure, consolidation, new leadership, or releasing new products, they invest in multiple communication platforms to clearly define the change and value to all stakeholders.

Company D has a top-notch Communication Department that strategically aligns key messages from an internal timing perspective to press releases. The leaders get out in front of the change, leverage the input of diverse teams, craft messages that clearly resonate with all employees, and train and prepare managers for managing local communications and fielding questions.

Communication platforms are varied, depending on the change communication and the audience. Platforms include: conference calls, webinars, video calls, local manager communications and FAQ's, and emails from the CEO or respective senior leader once the initial communication is delivered. All include contacts for further questions.

I personally admire this organization for their foresight on how to effectively execute change. But, most importantly, the senior leadership team is cognizant of the need to inspire the employees, paint a realistic picture of change, and highlight future opportunities and the value of change.

PLATFORMS FOR COMMUNICATION

There are multiple communication platforms to choose from and/or integrate when building your communication plan. As you think about the best way to communicate change to the organization, there are many things to consider. Who is your audience? What are you communicating? Who will communicate the change? Where are the employees located? Do you have virtual teams? How many platforms do you need to leverage to reinforce the message? What about mobile technology? How do you communicate with the external world? What about the shareholders?

While communication is part of the overall change strategy, you do not want to simply reduce communication to a process. Keep the message concise and include timelines and links to important information and contacts in your written communications. When communicating change, it is important that leaders recognize the impact of change on people and their personal lives.

As you narrow down the platforms for communication, you may want to categorize them as internal, external, collaborative, and support platforms. Internal communication platforms include emails, meetings, video calls, webinars, conference calls, intranet, voice messages, and text. External platforms include mobile (if employees use their own device), texts, press releases, and talent acquisition sites. Social media has become a very collaborative way to communicate and includes Facebook, LinkedIn, and Twitter, as well as internal collaborative sites. And, the support platform could include EAP (Employee Assistance Program), Help Desk, News Feed, and your CRM Software.

An example of how this might work is reflected in Table 3 below.

Table 3. Example of Defining Platforms for a Communication

Communication	Audience	Internal	External	Collaborative	Support
Initial Change Communication from the CEO	All Employees	Conference Call and E-mail			
External Announcement	Outside World		Press Release		
Internal Posting about the Change			Internal Employee Site		
Positions Impacted					EAP

BUILDING THE COMMUNICATION PLAN

A cross-functional group of individuals is typically assigned to identify key messages and audiences that need to be communicated to throughout the organization. This group consists of senior leaders, experts on the change, and representation from legal, human resources, and communications.

Following are a few tips to consider when planning and executing a communication plan.

1. It is always better to hear major change announcements from the CEO or senior leaders.

2. Employee meetings are a very effective way to announce change and then field questions from employees.

3. Employees receive so many emails today, that in order for an email to get noticed, it is suggested you highlight the importance in the subject line. For example: ACTION REQUIRED – MANDATORY EMPLOYEE MEETING – DATE.

4. When scheduling conference calls, be sure to reserve enough lines for all callers. There is nothing worse than causing panic because employees are unable to dial into the conference call.

5. Text messages and voice messages are better served for updates and reminders for action-related deadlines.

6. Given the number of virtual teams in the work environment today, video calls are an ideal way to include them in change communication announcements, if they are not close to a company location.

7. Providing key contact information and links to employees makes it easier for you and the employees to access information.

8. Having a newsfeed on the intranet to use for updates and a way to respond to process questions allows employees

to communicate with one another and share standard information.

9. From a collaborative communication standpoint, companies may elect to proactively share some level of information about the pending change on social media.

10. Sales will need to develop a communication plan that covers how customers will be communicated to about the change. Who will communicate to key accounts? When and how will you communicate with customers? How will you involve the sales organization? Will a letter be distributed to all customers?

A sample Communication Plan template is provided in Table 4 below. It can be modified to include other key information you want to track.

Table 4. Sample Communication Plan

Communication	Audience	Medium	Owner	Date	Status
Reorganization Announcement	All Employees	Conference Calls	CEO/VP Comm.	TBD	Message Drafted
Letter from CEO	All Employees	E-mail	CEO/VP Comm.	TBD	Drafted and in Review Process
Dept. Meetings	All Employees	Meetings	Dept. VP's	TBD	Planning Underway
Internal Posting	All Employees	Intranet	VP Comm.	TBD	Complete
Press Release	External	Press Release	CEO/VP Comm.	TBD	Being Reviewed by Board
Notification to Key Account Customers	Key Accounts	Calls Assigned to Executives	VP Sales/CEO	TBD	Assignments Underway
Notification to Customers	All Customers	Letter from CEO/VP Sales	VP Sales/CEO	TBD	Complete

THE EXECUTIVE TEAM

As we discussed in Chapter 1, the #1 fear of most executives is change. This makes sense: employees know that senior leaders approve change initiatives; so, employees expect to hear from the top of the house when major changes are taking place in the business. If someone else is communicating the change, it should be because the CEO or top executive is no longer with the company. Otherwise, it tends to create confusion and distrust as to why employees are not hearing the message directly from the CEO.

Change communication at the CEO level is about thinking strategically to get your ideas accepted. You represent the change, a better future, and the leader/influencer who will guide the company from Point A to Point D. Change is not limited to priorities and processes. The CEO's role goes much deeper and is accountable for retention of talent, engagement, influencing change, and helping people through change. This requires a strong executive presence and a leader who can communicate the right messages at the right time.

Employees will be listening to the CEO's messages, watching their body language, and looking for conflicting messages from the senior leadership team. That is why it is critical to follow PACC (Purpose, Audience, Clear, and Concise) when crafting messages, and stick to the script. Unfortunately, when people get nervous, they talk too much and end up saying things that are unintentional and not in the script. Then, the organization has to go into damage control mode.

Spend time thinking about your audience and communicating at a level that all employees can understand. There needs to be one consistent message that can be shared with everyone. Take time to think about change communications in the past and what worked well and what did not work well. If this is your first time managing through change, then follow PACC and make sure that you are comfortable with the message and can deliver it with confidence.

The intention of the message versus the impact will have a lot to do with how it is received and how well you are able to connect with the workforce regarding the change. No one really likes change. And, some employees will resist change, at all levels of the organization. But, change can be more readily accepted if employees are treated fairly, their leaders are honest about what is happening, and a concerted effort is made to listen to feedback and minimize the distractions.

I remember a situation where the company was contemplating closing a Division. There were a lot of rumors and uncertainty in the division. Finally, the CEO approved keeping the division open and having the Division President communicate that decision to the employees. But, two weeks later, the CEO decided to close the division, and the Division President was forced to stand in front of the employees again and tell them that the location was being closed and that 65 people were going to receive a severance package that day. It cost the CEO and the Division President their credibility and created an undercurrent of distrust throughout the region. This is a perfect example of why it is so important to have alignment across the organization and clearly understand the impact on people's lives.

To avoid having information filtered when it is communicated to the CEO, it is a good idea for the CEO to place calls to leaders within the organization during times of change. That way, the CEO hears first-hand how things are going with respect to the change. These calls reinforce the leader's support and commitment to working through change and listening to the organization.

IMPORTANCE OF INFORMAL LEADERS

Unlike Formal Leaders who have authority within the organization, there are the Informal Leaders who are highly respected by the workforce. They earn this respect through tenure, performance, loyalty, or perhaps supporting fellow co-workers.

In times of change, the Informal Leader can be invaluable to the organization. Depending on how they view the change, the veterans of the company with years of experience may stand up and share their story of how well the company has treated them over the years. If they agree with the change, they will help others move forward. If they disagree with the change or do not understand the change, then the Informal Leader could work against you.

Do not underestimate the Informal Leader who has built relationships over time and is trusted for their integrity by the workforce. I have seen these leaders stand up on their own for actions taken by the organization, such as layoffs and automation of jobs. But, I have also seen them use their power and influence to negatively influence employees to leave the organization or to lower productivity rates.

No matter how well you communicate, there will be ongoing questions about change. Informal Leaders can be very inclusive in their daily interactions with other employees. The influence and role of the Informal Leader is just something you need to be aware of in the change process. They will either work for you or against you, and it is not something that you can control.

COMMUNICATING TO CUSTOMERS

It is wise to plan to get out in front of the communication to customers so they hear the message of change from you and not the competition. The CEO, Sales Vice President, and Communications Department should strategize on the best way to reach out to key accounts, and the timing of this communication. In addition, there needs to be a communication to all customers to inform them of the change.

The competition thrives on companies being distracted by change. They can and will use this as a pitch when speaking with your customers. By planning ahead and scripting a message to customers, you arm your sales force with a standard message that prevents speculation and personal opinions from interfering with the customer relationship.

One way of handling the communication is to have senior executives assigned to contact key accounts by phone and then set up a meeting with them to discuss any concerns. The majority of customers can be contacted by the sales rep assigned to them. The sales rep can review the scripted message with the customer and then follow up with a standard letter from the CEO to be distributed to all customers.

This puts you out in front of the competition, and the customer prefers to hear from you what is happening versus the competition.

I worked in an organization where the leadership team did not understand the importance of communicating to the customer, and they fell victim to damage control later. There is no substitute for proactive communication when it comes to your customers.

WHAT ABOUT THE MEDIA?

Depending on the size of your company and the scale of the change event, you may or may not hear from the media. If you are one of the largest employers in the area, if you incur significant layoffs or location closures, or there is a crisis, you should be prepared for at least the local media to come knocking on your door or make a call into the business.

If you do not have a crisis or communication protocol in the company, it is wise to establish one at the corporate office. All employees should be trained on the protocol so that they know how to handle any and all inquiries from the media (press, radio, reporters, etc.). The contact for these types of events is typically public relations, communications, legal, or the senior leader in charge.

As part of your communication plan, you should also give some thought to how the change will be reflected on social media. Many companies have IT monitoring the web or have a social media listening protocol service to monitor information that is posted by your employees or others about the company.

Employees may post comments on social media about losing their jobs or strong opinions about the changes happening in the company. And, it is not uncommon to see negative reviews posted on Glassdoor after a restructuring takes place. In the event that employees are impacted, former employees may use social media as a way to vent.

In today's changing world, there is a lot to think about when it comes to communication. By building a comprehensive Communication Plan covering the change and training your employees, you will be better prepared to handle the internal and external questions that come your way.

COACHING QUESTIONS - Chapter 4

Below are some suggested Coaching Questions to consider when working through your "Communication" Strategy:

1. What is the purpose of the communication?
2. What are we communicating?
3. How much should we communicate?
4. What medium should we use to communicate the change?
5. When should we communicate the change?
6. What is the timeline for the change?
7. Who should be involved in laying out the Communication Plan?
8. Who is the primary person to lead the Communication Plan?
9. Who is the audience?
10. What internal resources do we have?
11. What external resources do we need?
12. What best practices do we have to rely on from previous change announcements?
13. How do we communicate to and train the managers?
14. Do we need FAQ's (Frequently Asked Questions)?

CHAPTER 5

NAVIGATION
WHERE ARE WE HEADED, ANYWAY?

I skate to where the puck is going to be, not where it has been.
~ Wayne Gretzky

HOW TO EFFECT CHANGE

Navigation starts with maneuvering the change journey. No matter how hard you try, you cannot stop the future. Change means letting go of the past and moving forward. A big step in the journey is to understand what is changing and to forget the way you "used to do it."

Companies and employees need to be agile in order to quickly adapt to change. Who do you follow? How do you stay afloat? How long will change go on? Change is disruptive and exhausting to most employees, but it can be exhilarating to some employees. It offers opportunity, innovation, and the freedom to get out from under the old regime.

Getting out of your comfort zone and finding the courage to move forward and embrace change is key to personal growth and opportunities. Finding your way in the sea of change is daunting at times. However, keeping an open mind and "rolling with the punches" during change will prevent you from being left behind.

LEADING CHANGE FROM THE TOP

There are three things the CEO can do to effectively guide change – Lead, Inspire, and Listen (LIL). The CEO sets the direction from a leadership, culture, and strategy perspective. She/he is accountable for moving the organization from where they are today to the future state of where they need to be. This dimension is known as the "white space." (Turner 2009).

The white space in many respects is the same concept as the white board that hangs on office walls and in conference rooms. The white board is used to map out ideas and processes to get from Point A to Point B. Some companies even incorporate the white board into their interview process, and candidates are sent to the white board to solve a problem. The white space and white board encourage innovative ideas and open up unlimited possibilities.

Instead of tweaking strategies and project plans, the CEO may want to consider "erasing the board" and starting over. Evaluating details versus exploring possibilities may be the cause of failure for many well-intentioned change initiatives. Leaders need to ask themselves:

— "What am I missing?"

— "Does my leadership team have the capacity to get the job done?"
— "How does the team rank on emotional intelligence?"

Executing change involves setting clear expectations, navigating the unknown, and having a strong leadership team in place. The CEO cannot execute alone. In order to successfully navigate the change journey, it is critical that the leadership team is capable of managing and developing their employees. The team's job is to execute the change strategy and deliver results. "Although the leader makes the decisions and defines the change event, it is the affected individuals that will ultimately determine whether it achieves the return on investment." (Turner 2009).

Part of the due diligence process, often overlooked, is evaluating the leadership capacity of the leadership team selected to execute the change. As we know from stories of failed change initiatives, just being financially savvy and having a plan does not necessarily lead to success. Part of the change process means evaluating your team and understanding skills gaps and their ability to influence and motivate others.

Understanding others is a key attribute when going through change. The emotionally intelligent leader is very self-aware of his/her attributes. Leaders high on emotional intelligence understand how to motivate others, have empathy for how employees feel during change, and they understand the importance of relationships and the role they play in the change process.

Plans do not guarantee success. Leaders will need to be prepared to manage through unforeseen crises and turns in the road that were unexpected. Despite all the planning and preparation for change, there will be details that were missed, programs that don't work, and unexpected employee challenges. But, placing a priority on the people side of the business and aligning it with the process side creates a roadmap for the journey.

The 2018 World's Top Two Most Innovative Companies, reported by *FAST Company*, were Apple and Netflix (The World's 50 Most Innovative Companies 2018). Apple CEO, Tim Cook, places an emphasis on products, people, and culture in guiding the vision of the company. Also, from a consumer perspective, his focus is on people and how they use the products. Apple understands that success is not just about innovation but a strong connection to the employees and consumers who drive the innovation and make the "cool" products.

Reed Hastings, CEO, President, and Chairman of the Board for Netflix, made an amazing recovery from his decision in 2011 to raise subscription prices 60 percent and split streaming and DVD services. That decision cost him 800,000 subscribers and saw a stock price plummet of 35 percent. He led a redesign of Netflix and repositioned the company as a film entertainment company catering to consumer niches (Garvey 2018).

Like Apple, Netflix places a strong emphasis on culture. Their culture values people over process, with values that revolve around independent decision-making, curiosity, passion, being selfless, innovation, and stimulating creativity.

One lesson to be learned from these two companies is that people and culture are a critical part of the innovation and change strategy. Instead of delegating culture to one of the functional areas, it is the CEO's responsibility to lead and protect the culture. And, the CEO is wise to listen to and seek out feedback from the organization to validate that the culture values are not being compromised.

As the company navigates change, the CEO will also be responsible for updates to the Board of Directors. By stepping outside the office and engaging in multiple touch points, the CEO is able to provide first-hand information and not rely on just the opinions of staff or to be unduly influenced by others.

It is not uncommon for the CEO to bring in outside resources to help support the change. Outside resources may be used to evaluate and develop leadership skills, supplement skill gaps, help build best practices, assist in system integrations, and provide expertise around business model evaluations and public relations. External resources can help provide an objective viewpoint along with challenging risks and opportunities in the change strategy.

There are many ways that the CEO navigates change. Navigation starts with selecting a strong senior leadership team and ideally supporting each member with an Executive Coach who will help them manage through difficult situations and behaviors. The CEO must evaluate the competitive landscape and time change events. Then, the CEO has to influence and sell change to the organization. Even more challenging, the CEO has to stay out in front of the change strategy and continue to evaluate and support the impact on the people side while evaluating how well the plan is working. They must constantly challenge themselves to understand what they are missing as the Captain of the Change Ship.

Successfully navigating change from the top is a huge undertaking by the CEO. The two primary reasons that change events fail are: (1) the lack of attention to the people side of change, and (2) the managers' lack of knowledge about the underlying theory and processes of change (Andrews, Cameron & Harris, 2008). A breakdown in communication is typically the cause when plans get off schedule and timelines are not met. The CEO is the strategist, the spokesperson, the leader, the people motivator, and the jack-of-all-trades when it comes to change.

CASE STUDY 6
TOXIC LEADERSHIP AND CULTURE

Only once in my career did I work for a company where I would call the culture toxic. Consider yourself lucky if you have not experienced this type of work environment. The culture was one of fear and almost debilitating for some of the employees.

On occasion, and when it benefited the senior leader, he could be charming. But, on most days, his staff and employees were afraid to speak up for fear they would be admonished in public. There was a lack of trust in the organization and an undercurrent that prevented collaboration and teamwork. And, there was a lot of gossiping and conversations behind closed doors for fear of being heard.

The focus was on processes, approvals, and titles versus consistent goals and accountability. Leaders found themselves highly frustrated and unable to do their jobs. Everything had to be approved and debated at the top, so few initiatives moved forward.

The company was dysfunctional by most standards with a reputation on the street of not being a place you wanted to work. Talent was hard to hire, and multiple employment agencies refused to collaborate. Once on board, many new hires became quickly disillusioned with the company.

With double standards at the top and exceptions to the rules, the turnover was high in professional positions, and the results reflected a steady decline. Employees spun their wheels trying to get their work done. Most employees respected the history of the company and talked about the possibilities of what it could be under a strong leader.

What happened next? After disastrous results and failure to deliver on promises, there was finally a change in leadership. This case study is an example of the approximately 50% of executives that fail to lead change in a new role. Not only is it important to provide support and coaching when an executive is new or struggling, but timely decisions need to be made if the leader is unable to deliver the results.

SURVIVAL OF THE FITTEST

Navigating change includes navigating the positioning and politics that surface when a company is experiencing change. Relationships play a big role in navigating change. Who is in charge? Who is creating the future? How do I survive? These are just a few of the questions that employees ask themselves when attempting to navigate the unknown.

The world you knew before is gone. The evolution can be painful, disorganized, and unclear in terms of who is in charge, and who will survive. But, the alternative is to opt out and leave the organization. To move forward means that you do not know whom to trust, there is jockeying for positions, and guaranteed back-stabbing that occurs.

Employees and managers feel challenged with high stress levels and surviving the change. No doubt there is a lot of unproductive behavior and positioning during times of change. But, change also represents an opportunity to contribute to the future and share your viewpoint: in fact, diverse viewpoints can be welcome during periods of change when management is looking for viable solutions. Take advantage of the opportunity to hear from different points of views.

While there are always people that play to win and are opportunists, change is really about a better way of doing things. And, if managed well, change is about respecting differences and contributing to a better tomorrow. Change can be a time to excel and offer new solutions. Changing direction with the proper guidance from the top of the organization can actually propel the company and industry into creating cutting-edge solutions.

Change initiatives should have a clear strategy that can be articulated to the organization. It is a given that employees will be challenged with the uncertainty of change. No one likes to live in a state of the unknown. It raises a lot of questions if employees do not receive regular updates on how the change is progressing. What is happening? Why have we not had an update? What did you hear? Will there be a change in senior leadership?

Successful change management should not be about the number of hours that you work as an employee or manager. Although, there are leaders who value the time you spend at the office versus the achievement of results. Successful change management is about working the plan and ensuring that managers and employees are armed with the tools and resources they need to survive the change.

ROLE OF THE MANAGER

Your role as a manager in an organization undergoing change will be challenging. In addition to your normal job, you can expect to deal with more employee questions and challenges and a heavier workload.

This is your opportunity to step up and be the change to help your organization cross the finish line. By increasing your communication with your team and keeping a pulse on how employees are handling change, you can keep your employees motivated and focused on getting the job done.

After the change announcement, it is important to talk to employees and identify which individuals are having the most anxiety and struggling with the change. Your job is not to be a therapist, but to provide support and direct individual employees to the right channel for support, answers, and help. There are Employee Assistance Programs, hotlines, and Human Resource Managers who should be able to guide you through this process.

The faster you can get employees refocused on their work, the better your chances are to stabilize productivity and help the team be successful. Eliminating fear, moving forward, and reinforcing support is a great start. Where there are significant changes involved, you will need to arrange for training and support. A good example of this is when new systems are involved or an integration occurs. Employees will need training and someone to help them develop new skills and master the process. This may mean bringing in experts to assist with the learning process.

Periodically, it is a good idea to do a self-evaluation as the leader. How am I doing? What are the competencies where I can improve? What am I doing to develop and support the team? What's not working? What are the possibilities?

You can also leverage change to help bond relationships within the team. Pairing up employees to help each other and providing team effectiveness training can really increase the success rate of initiatives. This can be highly beneficial when managing through chaos. Collaborative teams and team members play a significant role in preventing failure.

A great example of this was when I joined a company in a senior leadership role and had a team that was not highly regarded by the CEO. The goal was to create a strategy that aligned the people strategy with the business initiatives. Sounds simple enough. But, the team was used to working independently and reporting in to a Region leader. So, having the team report directly to me meant a lot of resistance.

Often, when a new leader arrives, many employees protect their turf and are skeptical. They fail to understand it is about the team and not about themselves.

Fortunately, one of my new staff members stepped up and provided a historical perspective along with her working knowledge of the organization and who's who to help me quickly transition into my role. The integrity, work ethic, and commitment of this individual were amazing.

The team brainstormed new approaches and we were able

to combine the old with the new to make progress and create collaboration across the globe. The team members voiced their viewpoints and concerns but also offered solutions. This was an important milestone in the journey since we needed team members to understand that they should feel free to offer suggestions and feedback and not just raise issues and problems.

In a relatively short period of time, this collaborative effort enabled the team to deliver results as we built and put our strategy into action. The team partnered with the business to find common ground and to make valued contributions versus pushing policy changes. Change was still challenging but workable.

Following are some tips for making change easier for employees:

1. Provide regular updates to employees in staff meetings or in a quick morning get together.
2. Refrain from over-complicating processes and work assignments.
3. Ensure that employees have the tools and resources to do the job.
4. Encourage employees to speak up and share constructive feedback.
5. Use change as a way to develop your employees and identify leaders.
6. Assign mentors to new hires or employees coming onboard from an acquisition.
7. Do not tolerate bad behaviors.
8. Model leadership behaviors.
9. Solicit employee volunteers to plan monthly luncheons or small events to recognize employee contributions.
10. Roll up your sleeves and LISTEN when the going gets tough.
11. Host a few lunches and learn to help employees manage stress and deal with change.
12. Understand that people learn in different ways (visual, written, simulations, on the job, etc.).

ROLE OF THE COACH

Executive coaching is a way to help individuals work through difficult decisions, challenges, or behavior changes to create sustainable change solutions. The coach can help you move from where you are today to where you want to be in the future.

Coaching opportunities span a wide variety of topics including the pain of growth, culture shifts, failed initiatives, restructuring, new leadership, developing leadership skills, and underperforming teams. Measurable outcomes are established for success. Outcomes can include: improving financial performance, accelerating change, taking your skills to the next level, improving the success rate of new leaders, and improving productivity.

The Executive Coach works with you to provide a clear understanding of strengths, limitations, leadership attributes, and development needs. A personal development plan is created to reflect clear expectations around what is being coached. The coach helps you explore insights and possibilities related to your coaching in a safe environment.

Some companies provide an external Executive Coach as part of their talent development program, while other companies have internal coaches. And, it is not uncommon for executives to hire their own Executive Coach. The key to success is maximizing the value of the coaching engagement through your commitment to the process.

Relationships are key, so chemistry between you and your coach is imperative. It is recommended that you have a certified and experienced Executive Coach who is able to successfully guide you through the process to achieve your desired outcome(s). Ultimately, the goal is to improve your capabilities and build capacity in your current or future leadership roles.

In times of change, the Executive Coach serves as an unbiased resource that can help you work through the best outcome. The coach pushes you to explore the possibilities and next steps in the journey. Many times, as an executive, we know the answer, but need the coach to help us think through the options and develop an action plan.

The Executive Coach can be an invaluable confidante to executives and eliminate the fear of the unknown. It is lonely at the top, and senior executives often find themselves in a situation with no one to bounce ideas off of. As you build trust with the coach and see results, coaching becomes a great way to develop skills and change behaviors. The outcome can be highly beneficial to your career and to the business.

CASE STUDY 7
NOT APPROACHABLE

As an executive, it is important to get out of your office and stay in touch with what is going on in the organization, especially during times of change. I worked with two executives who were brilliant workers but stayed in their office with the door shut all day studying the numbers. The financials are definitely important, and delivering results is part of the accountability that goes along with the job. But, they became viewed as unapproachable because they did not build relationships in the organization and did not support or communicate well with their teams.

Both executives suffered from the same problem – they wanted to be the smartest person in the room. You always felt like you were being asked trick questions as opposed to engaging in a conversation where there could be a learning opportunity for both parties. This kind of behavior is de-motivating, even manipulative, and does not build loyalty.

In both cases, other leaders would call me and ask when the CEO was coming out to visit their location to meet the employees and learn more about the business. But, despite feedback to the executives, they felt that these requests were not a good use of their time. They delegated meetings and travel to other members of the team and continued to allow their introverted personality to be an excuse. But, people wanted to hear from the CEO.

Both executives had Executive Coaches. They were coached on communication and building relationships. One of the executives in this case study lost the respect of his team and was ultimately replaced when he did not deliver the results. The other executive built a relationship with the Board of Directors, continued to grow in his role, and successfully delivered results.

It is possible that as a leader you can stay in your office and still deliver the results, with a great team around you. I would not recommend this approach. However, your reputation as a senior leader may also be viewed as an elitist who only shows up for key events. Learning how to balance financial accountability with people accountability was an opportunity for the executives in this case study. And, when executives are not committed, they cannot be coached.

WE'RE IN THIS TOGETHER

Do your employees see themselves as struggling through change as an individual, or have you provided a roadmap for them to feel connected to the change and each other. Are they a collaborative team working toward the same goal? Or, are they siloed and worried about how they survive?

When employees understand the change and how their role contributes to the success of the change, they are more likely to feel engaged and collaborate with their fellow co-workers. If the senior executive is successful at creating a compelling vision, which clearly outlines the benefits of change, employees can be connected to a common cause.

Everyone has connections, but not everyone builds relationships with those connections. Connections can be people that we know but do not know well. If leaders can influence employees to collaborate in the work environment on projects and initiatives to deliver the change, then previous "connections" become a "relationship." That co-worker now becomes someone that we share memories with and bond with by working through change together. That relationship may translate into a lifetime friend with whom we share a common bond.

I would argue that if more leaders would build strong teams that are empowered, the possibilities of innovative ideas could be leveraged to create team bonds that deliver growth through the diversity of thought. However, when a leader feels the need to control and micromanage, they are limiting the experiences and commitment gained through collaboration.

When employees feel connected to the cause, the challenges they face do not seem as daunting because they feel the support from the organization and their co-workers. Employees can be inspired to be ambassadors for change and eliminate the feeling of "going it alone."

The agility of an organization can also help when it comes to change. If the structure, roles, and infrastructure are agile, the organization can quickly navigate and work through change. If an organization is overly complex in its structure, systems, processes, and hierarchy, then it becomes far more difficult for the organization to change course. An example of this is turnaround companies where there is a limited time that the leadership team has to restructure and get to profitability.

Strong leadership teams, like those at Apple and Netflix, place a value on the people side of the equation. By leading, inspiring, and listening (LIL), leaders set the pace for the journey. They connect employees to the cause, empower, and have high expectations. But, employees are more engaged with the process and can see the light to the finish line.

COACHING QUESTIONS - Chapter 5

Below are some suggested Coaching Questions to consider when working through your "Navigation" Strategy:

1. How can we successfully navigate this change?
2. What skills do I need to develop?
3. What skills are missing on the leadership team?
4. What resources does the team need?
5. How do I create a safe environment?
6. How do I connect employees to a common cause?
7. When will they let go of the past?
8. What am I missing?
9. Where should my time be spent?
10. How do I address unproductive behaviors?
11. How do employees feel about the change?
12. How do I make the change easier for employees?
13. How can I more effectively communicate updates?
14. What is working?
15. What is not working?

CHAPTER 6

REINVENTION
FROM CATERPILLAR TO BUTTERFLY

hrthought
CHANGE MODEL

FEAR OF CHANGE

BENEFITS OF CHANGE

REINVENTION
Change or be
left behind

DISRUPTION

COMMUNICATION   NAVIGATION

Change is the law of life and those who look only to the past or present are certain to miss the future.
~ John F. Kennedy

TRANSFORMATIONAL CHANGE OR NEW DIRECTION

Reinvention is the stage in the change curve where it is time to fully integrate the elements of the change strategy. This is where the future state of the organization meets the final alignment of the steps to get there. It requires a final push from the CEO to communicate the clarity of the remainder of the journey.

In many ways, reinvention is the beginning of the recovery process and a rebalancing act to incorporate the vision into the culture. This is where the question can be answered as to whether the change was a complete transformation versus a new direction for the organization.

Transformational change typically constitutes a massive overhaul of the organization structure and strategy. Examples of this would be rolling out a new supply chain business model or, shifting a culture from non-enterprising to entrepreneurial. On the other hand, a new direction change could be spawned by changes in leadership, tweaks to the business model, restructuring, or consolidation of the business.

Whether change is labeled transformational or taking a new direction, the CEO is Responsible For The Future (RFTF) with a focus on executing the final steps of the strategy. This includes leveraging the company's new vision, role changes, developing skills, digital innovation, and beginning to explore new horizons.

At this point, the epitome of change itself is to leave the disruption behind and concentrate on the priorities for tomorrow, while highlighting the new changes and connecting talent to the vision. Having navigated the earlier stages of change, it is now time to dismiss the old way of doing things and welcome the future and the benefits of change.

CULTIVATING A REINVENTION MINDSET

Whether we like to admit it or not, everyone is vulnerable and occasionally finds themselves in a situation where they lack confidence or feel uncomfortable. The ability to face change with confidence increases with experience, both personally and from a career perspective.

Reinvention requires an open mindset and embracing new opportunities. Change is often full of cryptic messages early on, but now is the time for leaders to be transparent about the changes to come. Successful leaders understand the importance of executing not only the process and structure changes but also being sensitive and respectful as it relates to people.

In its simplistic form, reinvention is about executing a growth strategy for the organization. How well the CEO handles the reinvention stage of change as it relates to the people will be amplified across the organization. So, it is critical to think about the needs of the people beyond today. Talent is not a program, and it can quickly take a detour called "turnover" if not effectively communicated and accepted.

Executing a bold vision requires strong influence skills at the top of the organization and the ability to lead the way through reinvention as you integrate the new changes. Leaders must be prepared for resistance but ultimately be prepared to get their ideas accepted by the organization while building a coalition of support from within.

As leaders move from "Caterpillar to Butterfly," they need to be prepared to effectively communicate to the organization with (PACC) – Purpose, Audience, Clear, and Concise messages – to cultivate a reinvention mindset in the organization that understands that change has ups and downs and touches people's lives.

WHAT DOES TOMORROW'S LEADER LOOK LIKE?

As the older generation retires, I think we will see a significantly different type of leader emerge to lead organizations. The next generation leader will be more globally astute, expect diversification of the workforce, have grown up with technology, and have limited tolerance for the "way we used to do things." They will potentially be less verbally communicative to the organization but be better prepared to relate to the needs of employees. Tomorrow's leader will be focused on teams and less on building hierarchies that slow down productivity and drive inefficient business models.

I see the leader of tomorrow being culturally astute, leveraging generational differences, throwing out the old "employee handbooks" and possibly downsizing and redeploying the HR function as a strong Organization Development Team while potentially parceling out the transactional pieces to other functional areas. The opportunity awaits this leader for increased automation, simplification of policies and practices, driving an agile business model, and promoting more flexibility to the workforce as a way to attract and retain talent in a Gig economy.

The talent strategy will shift to accommodate more remote, temporary, and contract workers, given the entrepreneurial aspiration of many employees. Likewise, there will be continued pressure from workers to provide a more liberal family leave benefit and to lobby for a solution for a broken healthcare model and rising costs. And, the talent strategy will focus on succession planning, developing leadership skills, and career paths for the next generation. The leader of tomorrow will clearly understand the importance of investing in talent versus the previous generation's trend of cost-cutting in this area.

Change has become a way of life in organizations and is no longer an isolated event or a training program. It is a constant dynamic in the work environment and must become integrated into the culture so that leaders are prepared to manage change with minimal disruption. Instead of creating barriers and limitations, change can be revolutionary—supported by a strong talent strategy and empowerment across the organization.

Given the recent trend we are seeing with companies adding more women to boards and appointing more women to senior level positions, I would be remiss not to address what I believe will be the impact of this change across organizations.

Catalyst Inc. has reported for years that companies with more female representation delivered better financial results. Catalyst's research showed that, "Companies with the most women board directors had a 16% higher return on sales than those with the least, and a 26% higher return on invested capital." (Catalyst 2017). "MSCI found that three or more women change boardroom dynamics substantially and enhance the likelihood that women's voices and ideas are heard." (Catalyst 2017). In the same study, it was found that companies with few women on boards had more governance-related controversies (Catalyst 2017).

Despite this research, there is still only a small percentage of women that hold top corporate leadership positions. According to the fact tank, Pew Research Center, women only held about 10% of the top executive roles in companies in the United States in 2016-2017. In U.S. companies, women make up 5.1% of CEO's, 11.2% of CFO's, 23.7% of general counsel positions, and 10% were chief human resources officers (DeSilver 2018).

It begs the question of what is holding back female leaders from breaking the glass ceiling that has been talked about for years. Is the work environment, as many women suggest, still a good old boys club? "Is gender bias still obstructing the leadership identity development for women?" as suggested in Women Rising: The Unseen Barriers (Ibarra, Ely, and Kolb 2013). Are women supporting and elevating other women enough? And, is this identify shift changing as a result of generational differences with female Millennials pushing harder for equality?

In 2015, Pew Research Center published an article, "What Makes a Good Leader, and Does Gender Matter?" The survey concluded that the essential leadership traits that matter the most are: Honesty, Intelligence, Decisiveness, and Organization. There were gender gaps identified as it related to the leadership traits of Compassionate, Innovative, and Ambitious. Women were seen as more compassionate and innovative, while men were seen as more ambitious. But, to the extent that the public felt these gender differences were essential or mattered in terms of who would make a better leader, there was little difference (Pew Research Center 2015).

My opinion differs as it relates to the essential leadership traits that make a good leader. In tomorrow's work environment, I think the key leadership traits are: Integrity, Developing People, Strategic Vision, Innovation, Results Orientation, and Self-Awareness. And, it is important to take gender out of the equation in the future as it relates to leadership.

The past stereotypes of women that limited their upward mobility are being challenged today. We must move beyond the notion that women "take care" and men "take charge." This limiting and dated mindset does not belong in the corporate environment of today. Coaching women to develop male tendencies and to downplay their femininity, dress, and viewpoints is outdated. The identify shift will help organizations move from viewing female leaders as aggressive when they are actually being assertive. This means that old school coaches will need to change their methodologies and get aligned with the new leaders and work environment.

I believe that the impact of the increasing representation of female leaders in the workplace will result in an improved work-life blend, investing in employee development, collaboration and team effectiveness, a focus on developing female leaders, high integrity, and more efficiently run organizations. We don't need a movement to do that: we need to recognize and reward talent irrelevant of gender and ethnicity.

The following article that I wrote in 2018 is being included since it is intended to help females work through change.

THE COURAGE TO EXCEL AS A WOMAN

Having the courage to excel, as a woman, starts with being willing to face your fears, speaking up for what is right, allowing yourself to be vulnerable, and leveraging the possibilities on the tough road ahead. Courage carries with it a certain level of risk and vulnerability. It signals that you can lean into change and embrace change dynamics. It also means that you are willing to set and attain higher goals and take ownership of your career.

So, where does this courage come from? Why do some people seem to have courage and others do not? In many cases, females that have courage attribute it to having strong women in their lives, strong leaders and role models (men or women), being raised to believe that they could aspire to do better and be more because it was possible, or being the oldest in the sibling lineup. They were raised to be independent and to "Believe that you can," which ultimately translated into confidence and drive for many of them.

I have coached a lot of professional women over my career. Some of them attributed their lack of courage and confidence to:

1) Not having the positive reinforcement experienced by other women
2) The way female-identified people are socialized
3) The culture and the historical male dominance in the workplace
4) Implicit bias

Developing confidence and learning to be more assertive has been a developmental focus for them and other females as they progressed their career.

For a start, women need to set their own standards and realize that success comes from accepting that it is all right to feel, think, and be different from men. In fact, this thought process drives inclusion and reinforces diversity. Stop trying to be someone that you are not, stop mimicking male behaviors and tendencies, and strive for the courage to break down the status quo. In essence, stop trying to fit a square peg into a round hole.

True leaders are authentic and realize that in life, each of us has to make choices. The choice for women should not be whether you can have a career or a family. You can have either or both, and it is your choice. You can aspire to be a physician, a top role in Corporate America, or decide to have a more balanced approach. Whatever you choose, the choice revolves around finding a work-life blend. Prioritizing what is important to you and finding quality time for yourself is really important. There are trade-offs, but with a little planning and prioritization, you can find the appropriate work-life blend that allows you to excel.

It takes courage and tenacity to follow your dream and not give up when you run into roadblocks, or the journey gets tough. The journey to success builds character and makes you a stronger person and leader. Sometimes, you have to take an unexpected detour to achieve your goals, relocate, or make a vertical move to get there. Years ago, a mentor of mine told me that, "Successful people do things other people won't." By this, he meant that I should be open to opportunities that represented advancement, exposure to global experiences, and do not limit my options. This was great advice and helped me to carefully consider and evaluate each career step to make sure it aligned with my goals and broadened my professional experience.

Women admit that they tend to create self-imposed stress and worry too much about how they are perceived. Many of the females I have coached felt that they had to work twice as hard as a male colleague to get the recognition they deserved. Did they, or were they imposing higher standards on themselves? Learning and growing as a professional means that you are going to experience failure at some point and make mistakes. The feeling of failure is inevitable at some point since we are human and not perfect. So, it is important to find a way to alleviate that stress, maintain a sense of humor, and rebound with renewed experience, confidence, and a healthy competitive drive.

Thus, the importance of a Support Network that you can trust when you need to work through issues, develop new skills, and have someone who can relate to your challenges. This network can be a group of female professionals, a mentor (male or female) or a coach that creates a safe environment for you. This network can help you validate what you are thinking, open up new possibilities, and create positive reinforcement combined with constructive feedback. This network is very valuable and helps prevent failure and/or the urge to give up.

One thing is for certain, the courage to excel comes from within, sticking to your values, and making a commitment to support other females. You have to believe that you can achieve your goals and drive for excellence. Ultimately, the journey is that females will see themselves as and be viewed as, professional, without the reference to gender. You are paying it forward for your children, grandchildren, and the next generation that promises to deliver even more equality.

WHAT DOES THE WORK ENVIRONMENT OF THE FUTURE LOOK LIKE?

The traditional work environment is a thing of the past and is being heavily influenced by a growing Gig economy and telecommuting benefits to employees and companies. Other factors influencing this change include: the talent shortage, people working longer and delaying retirement, 24/7 connectivity, longer commute times, entrepreneurial aspirations of workers, and an increasing demand from workers for a better work-life blend.

The Gig economy offers a larger talent pool of expertise to employers and autonomy and flexibility to workers. It is also less expensive for companies to hire part-time workers, temps, contractors, and consultants, which represent a growing number of "non-employee" types today.

This trend also drives a social change in the work environment. Instead of seeing work as a part of your social network, work now offers less one-on-one interaction and raises the bar for talent. It provides employers with another resource to find specific skills for specific projects. It means that more people will continue to work remotely and at home.

In the September 2018 edition of *The Economist*, it was predicted that even Silicon Valley will "become more of an idea instead of a place, and will be geographically diversified." This will accommodate talent leaving the valley and result in smaller offices in other geographically desirable areas. Workers will be connected to the culture through messaging, video-conferencing and collaborating online.

Combine the Gig economy trend with technology, and the new work environment may result in leadership and accountability challenges for companies, along with a less structured work environment. Employees are demanding more flexibility. So, it is likely that we will continue to see the evolution of this new way of working in the future. With portable devices and telecommuting options, there is no reason for people to go to the office every day.

In fact, according to Global Workplace Analytics, 25% of employees are engaged in "teleworks" at some frequency today. And, it is estimated that approximately 50% of employees hold a job that is compatible with telecommuting. As of 2017, 3.2% (or 4.3 million employees) now work from home at least half the time (Globalworkplaceanalytics.com 2018). It is important to note that these statistics do not include self-employed workers.

The trend of telecommuting is expected to continue to rise in the future. It offers benefits to both employees and employers. Telecommuting statistics estimate that companies can save $11,000 per telecommuter every year. And, they are revamping their workspaces around the fact that "employees are already mobile and away from their desk 50-60% of the time." The additional upside for telecommuters is that it can save an estimated $2,000 – $7,000 per year in other expenses.

Telecommuters have reported being happier, more productive, more engaged, better able to manage their life, they take fewer sick days and are less stressed. This is a benefit that most Fortune 1000 Companies offer to their employees. Full-time employees are four times more likely to have work-at-home options than part-time workers (Globalworkplaceanalytics.com 2018). These remote workers seem to be drawn to coffee shops, hotel lobbies, and cafes to conduct their business. Workers want more control of their life, and this flexible arrangement offers a way to do just that.

For the offices that remain, it appears that the long despised "office cubicle" will remain. As a rule, it offers no privacy and decreases productivity, but it is cost effective. Perhaps the height of the cubicle walls will get a little higher, and they can still be sold as "promoting collaboration."

The work environment of the future is like choosing from a menu every day. Workers can choose where they sit and conduct their work, how they connect to the organization, the technology they use, the team they work with, the company they work for, and when they work. There are standing desks, modern break rooms with amenities like you'd see in cafes, collaborative spaces, quiet rooms, nap rooms, and multiple large screens that stream updates and messages.

However, companies are faced with a potential leadership breakdown today as they rush to close leadership skill gaps and prepare tomorrow's leaders to manage the new workplace challenges. With all the focus on collaboration, there appears to be a disconnect with holding people accountable for their deliverables. In some cases, relationships are getting in the way, and in others, finding the talent to replace someone is a big challenge.

A lot of emphasis has been placed on the correlation of onboarding to retention of employees over the past few years. What about the employee experience tomorrow? How will onboarding and training be handled? With a growing Gig economy, what will be the impact on antiquated policies and benefits? With more remote and contract workers, will the company overview and culture dynamics become more robotic or dropped entirely for these workers? There is certainly the risk of the work environment becoming more impersonal, less social, and creating a disconnect between the work being done and the overarching business strategy.

How will managers communicate effectively with employees? What about performance management? Will it continue to move to an online multi-feedback process that results in spending less time in a structured review process coaching and career planning with the employee? Or, will organizations recognize communication as a way to build engagement and place a stronger emphasis on coaching and mentoring to develop and retain talent?

With more remote workers, collapsing hierarchies, and a focus on teams in the workplace, companies may need to consider shifting their employee engagement focus to team engagement. The old mindset of trying to connect employees to the company and creating loyalty is no longer a viable strategy. Instead, there is a ripe opportunity to connect employees to smaller groups and teams where they tend to establish a bond today. Teams offer an avenue where you can share ideas, make friends, and get support and immediate gratification for your accomplishments.

Let's not forget the importance of an individual's network today that extends well beyond the walls of the work environment. Social media provides access to a global network of friends, colleagues, and 2nd degree connections just waiting to be tapped for expertise and to become part of a social broadcast.

With employees dictating more of the terms of their employment, there appears to be a shift of power to the employee side of the equation where they have the sought-after skills, and they are advising employers what needs to be done from a work perspective versus senior leaders dictating the direction of change.

So, the work environment of the future is trending toward being more casual and informal with a focus on creating a collaborative space (internally or externally) where employees can be innovative and empowered while striving for work-life blend.

HOW ARE EMPLOYEES IMPACTED DURING REINVENTION?

As organizations enter the Reinvention Wheel of Change, most employees have moved from fear of change to the reality of change. That does not mean that employees are anxiety-free. It often means workers see the "writing on the wall" and have a pretty solid idea of the future direction of the company.

Overall, employees have become accustomed to organizations restructuring and the resulting effect on employees. And, unfortunately, it has made employees less loyal to organizations. As a result, younger employees do their job, receive a paycheck, get as much experience as they can, and they move on to the next opportunity.

As companies reinvent themselves, now and in the future, employees are learning how to adapt and what skills are highly valued. Astute employees have an internal network that keeps them posted on the politics in the organization and changes that may be lurking behind closed doors. Simply put, that means that at least 60-70% of the workforce is looking for a job, and recruiters know that. But, most employees need a job to pay their bills, so you can't blame them for looking out for themselves. They would rather leave and find a job versus being restructured out of the organization.

As companies are willing to pay more to attract talent,

employees become more open to making a move to increase their compensation and provide a better standard of living for themselves and their families. The job market is more competitive today, and companies are challenged to find talent.

Employee development is at the top of the list for Millennials, but it is estimated that only 40% of companies are investing in development. So, employees are taking advantage of YouTube, free tutorials on LinkedIn, and online modules and webinars to develop their skills. In essence, they are preparing themselves for the next interview, and often on the employer's nickel. Valued skills include: leadership, communication, financial, software applications, and project management.

As employees recognize the impact of change, they also work to reinvent themselves to remain competitive in the job market. Reinventing includes enhancing a wide variety of skills (i.e., technology, leadership, finance, executive presence, physical fitness, and updating one's personal appearance).

Change is always difficult for employees. Helping them find a path to success and alleviating the stress that comes with change means that leaders need to get involved to prevent morale issues and loss of productivity. Getting involved can be as simple as creating fun events to offset the stress, recognizing employee contributions, and carefully planning and communicating the timing of change.

Reinvention dictates that it is wise to timely communicate regarding future changes to the workforce to ensure a smooth transition. It gives employees time to be trained and prepare for their new role. It allows the leader time to build the team and ensure the necessary resources. And, it maps out an exit strategy that treats employees fairly and with respect. Your employer brand is very important to keep intact. Therefore, how you are perceived to treat employees in times of change will be captured on social media and communicated to multiple networks.

The Society of Human Resources published an engagement survey in 2017 that covered "Employee Job Satisfaction and Engagement" (SHRM 2017). In that survey, they found that the top five contributions to employee job satisfaction were:

1) Respectful Treatment
2) Overall Compensation
3) Trust Between Employees and Senior Leadership
4) Job Security
5) Opportunity to Use Skills and Abilities

It is important to note that only 33% of employees surveyed indicated that they were very satisfied with the level of trust with senior leadership. This highlights the fact that change can negatively impact engagement in an environment where employees have low trust when it comes to leadership in their organization. And, two out of five employees indicated that they would be open to looking for a new opportunity outside of their company within the next year.

All of this adds up to the need to carefully plan the people impact of a change event. Organizations not only touch employees' lives but also the lives of their families when they are impacted by change. To minimize the impact of change and to focus on building engagement, employers would be wise to recognize the above factors related to engagement and to capitalize on them for the purpose of attracting and retaining key talent.

The worker of the future will need to be empowered, independent, results driven and collaborative in order to navigate the obstacles of the evolving work environment. Their success lies in the value they bring to the organization, whether as an employee or non-employee. It is most likely, that in the Era of Disruption, workers will continue to postulate change.

Finally, in a world of constant change, I encourage all workers to take a pause once in a while and slow down to benefit from teachable moments to help and support other co-workers. There is value and payback when you stop and take the time to care about others.

CASE STUDY 8
THE POWER OF REINVENTING YOURSELF

Given the pace of change in today's work environment, many employees have been impacted by restructuring activities. It also means that reinvention is not limited to companies but that many individuals have been forced to reinvent themselves.

People are working longer today and delaying retirement due to necessity or the desire to keep busy and stay employed. This represents an opportunity for employers to expand their talent pool while capitalizing on the retention of knowledge and dedication in their workforce. It represents a tradeoff and commitment to invest in and develop skills while reaping the benefits of a generation that comes to work every day and values their job.

However, workers over 50 get stereotyped as "older" and unfortunately represent many of the employees who are restructured during change. Therefore, skills and staying at the top of your game becomes even more critical for these individuals. Proactively taking responsibility for developing your skills and "reinventing" yourself can play a significant role in survival in the workplace.

A good friend of mine is a perfect example of someone who successfully reinvented herself during a time when her company was going through a lot of change. She was employed as a Systems Analyst at a company where she had worked for 25 years. During that time, she saw the company experience the best of times and then begin experiencing a downward spiral based on the failure of senior leadership to invest in new technology and keep up with the industry.

The company had offered stable employment over the years and had a highly tenured workforce. At its peak, the employee benefits and perks were among the best in the industry. The company had a great reputation and a sizable applicant pool. Employees stayed based on career opportunities, culture, and perks (free lunch, flexible hours, and fun team building events). While she could have pursued employment outside of the company, it was overall a great place to work obviously, and all of sudden she had been there for 25 years.

Things started to change when the CEO left to take a new position. An inexperienced executive was named internally, and over the next few years, the company felt like it was treading water. Executives were complacent, the company was not growing, and the company started a quarterly cost-cutting initiative. Morale tanked, and employees were faced with uncertainty. The company lost some employees who decided not to stick around. However, given the tenure of employees, many thought the CEO would turn the company around.

After lackluster results over multiple years, the CEO resigned, and a new CEO was appointed. He replaced the existing executive team with his cronies and at higher salaries. Meanwhile, employees were not getting bonus checks based on the financial results. And, the new CIO announced that they would be upgrading their system, which meant that her expertise would no longer be needed at some point.

This was an eye opener for my friend to get moving. After some coaching, she approached her manager and volunteered to learn the new system, even if it meant doing so on her own time. She also told the CIO that she was interested in moving to a Business Analyst position and would be willing to travel and assist with system conversions. She was invited to attend the classes offered internally and also spent a lot of her own time learning advanced functions. She took the initiative to present training sessions and to exhibit her knowledge of the business and customer processes and reporting.

In this case, her ability to proactively reposition herself and upgrade her skills led to a promotion to a Quality Analyst. She went from plugging along as a Systems Analyst in her cubicle in an 8-5 job to being viewed as a valuable resource to step up and assist the company through a major change. This promotion also gave her the opportunity to travel and add international experience to her resume.

Today, she has worked through six conversions and is a sought-after resource. The company has yet another new CEO and is focused on a new business model. But, at this point, she is more confident than ever in her role and her ability to seek new employment, if necessary, or be a key contributor if the company is acquired.

I share this story because she is a great example of someone who had the foresight and tenacity to upgrade her skills and find a way to remain competitive within her company and the industry. She is an inspiration and role model to others who are faced with uncertainty every day. It required extra effort on her part and stress along the way, but the alternative was to have her position eliminated and struggle to market herself. The lesson learned for all of us is to "never give up" and not be afraid to reinvent yourself and speak up.

FROM EXECUTIVE TO ENTREPRENEUR

As I thought about multiple examples of reinvention that I have seen over the years, I landed on sharing my personal experience with my readers. So, this is for those of you who have a dream that lives outside of corporate America.

A little over two years ago, I was a Fortune 500 Executive and thought I was living the dream – big paycheck, title, and lots of achievements on my resume. I walked in one day only to be told that the company was going in a different direction and that my position was being impacted. I don't need to tell many of you, who have gone through the same experience, how shocking that was. The initial reaction was disbelief, and what do I do now.

Given time to think about the change, I realized that I had a lot of opportunities and focused on securing employment with a multinational company where I could capitalize on my background and experience. I landed a great opportunity with a company that was going through a cultural transformation and needed help creating their people strategy. It presented itself as an awesome opportunity until I realized that the promises that were made to me could not be kept based on the company's financial position. Ultimately, I made the decision to go from Corporate Executive to Entrepreneur.

Founding hrthought, LLC was a life-long dream that enabled me to move from a corporate strategist to a thought leader to help companies leverage change through the benefit of their leaders and their teams. It gave me the freedom to get away from the daily corporate politics and focus on best practices. I was able to use my leadership skills and business mind to explore the possibilities of helping companies and executives work through change and grow their business.

An executive coach once told me that I should remember to find quality time to think through things because I was good at creating strategies. However, when you are caught up in the daily challenges of corporate America, you don't often find that time. Today, I happier than ever and able to advise people and create change through my blog, my book, social media, my network, and individuals like you.

The value of what I do today is helping others, coaching individuals and teams through challenges, and shifting the mindsets of the future. There is nothing more gratifying than helping people achieve success.

COACHING QUESTIONS - Chapter 6

Below are some suggested Coaching Questions to consider when working through your "Reinvention" Strategy:

1. How do I create a "reinvention" mindset?
2. What are the gaps in the talent strategy?
3. How do we develop employees for the future?
4. What competencies do we need for leaders in the future?
5. How can my team benefit from coaching?
6. What challenges do we face as we roll out the new business model?
7. How do we create a coaching culture?
8. What is changing about our work environment?
9. What is the impact of technology on employees?
10. How do I communicate the changes to our customers?
11. How do I leverage generational differences?
12. What knowledge do I need to protect?
13. What policies need to be replaced?
14. What is the plan to support the new roles in the organization?
15. What is the impact of more female leaders in the organization?
16. What is our diversity and inclusion strategy?

CHAPTER 7

BENEFITS OF CHANGE
A BETTER TOMORROW

When you're finished changing, you're finished.
~ Benjamin Franklin

MEASURING THE EFFECTIVENESS OF THE CHANGE PROCESS

Now, it is time to measure the success of the change you just implemented. This is referred to as a Stakeholder Analysis. Comparing the actual results of the change initiative against the original defined goals and metrics that were set upfront will provide you with a picture of the overall effectiveness of the change and the impact on the stakeholders.

A few questions worth considering:

- Did you achieve the objectives that you established for justifying the change?
- Did the change provide the anticipated ROI?
- Is the model delivering the savings?
- Were all the identified costs/expenses taken out of the model, why/why not?
- How did the customers benefit from the change?
- Will the change increase the top and bottom line?
- How do you line up with the competition after the change?
- What remains to be done?
- How is employee morale?
- Were all milestones completed on time and within budget?

Measuring the success of change includes reviewing both qualitative and quantitative results. Qualitative measurements will determine if the activities and milestones in the project plan were actually completed. This analysis should also include looking at setbacks and analyzing the gaps so you understand what worked and what did not work. Engagement surveys fall into this category and can be a useful tool to gather feedback from employees. Other areas to review include training program preparation and completion, skill gap closures, and organization changes.

The quantitative analysis will involve looking at financial goals and key metrics to understand the success of the implementation and execution of the change process. Examples of quantitative goals include analyzing: YOY sales growth, customer retention, profitability improvement (GM $'s and GM %), actual spend-against budget, revenue/employee improvement, capital expenditure budget, and other defined targets.

A final report is typically prepared for review with senior leaders and Board members to provide them with a final overview and summary of the results. Included in this report are the qualitative and quantitative results, a section covering legal compliance and risks, and a report out on how the company's performance compares to benchmarks and best practices in the industry.

This chapter is designed to take a look at ideas on how to evaluate and conduct a post-change review. An example of a way to capture this information in a simple format is found at the end of this chapter.

LESSONS LEARNED

It is strongly recommended that companies have a standard operating practice in place to sit down with the leadership team and other key players to review and critique the overall execution of change initiatives. Many companies make this a practice, but I have worked for companies that did not conduct a comprehensive review against the actual results. They missed using this opportunity as a learning platform for future changes.

Lessons learned will vary, depending on the type and scale of the change initiative the organization executed. Some of the common lessons learned in companies I worked for included:

1) Unrealistic time frames to complete projects
2) Not building in time to resolve system errors
3) Gaps in processes, failure to communicate to all parties involved, skill gaps
4) Conflicting cultures
5) Failure to retain key talent
6) Underestimating the competition
7) Under-resourced projects
8) Relying too heavily on the opinion of a select few
9) Not preparing managers for change

One of the lessons that many leaders in companies learn during change is the value of teamwork in the organization. Team effectiveness increases efficiency, helps spread out the work, offers diverse experiences and skills, and helps the project stay on schedule. My mom always said that "two heads are better than one."

What comes to light for many companies today are that they are not prepared from a succession plan standpoint. In addition, they are weak from an organization development skill set, and the leaders in this area do not have experience working through complex change initiatives. While this may vary by company, I read somewhere that the average tenure of an Organization Development professional in companies today is approximately six years. Change is no longer a training program, but a constant priority for the CEO. This is clearly an area where companies need strong functional expertise, or they will need to supplement with outside organization development professionals.

The outcome of lessons learned should be documented as well as reviewed with the appropriate personnel and used to educate and build knowledge for the future. When organizations take the time to learn from change and institutionalize the knowledge versus claiming success all around, they are better positioned to prevent failure for future changes.

Conrad Hilton is quoted as saying, "Achievement seems to be connected with action. Successful men and women keep moving. They make mistakes, but they don't quit."

The leaders of successful organizations are willing to learn from failure, and they build stronger teams for the future.

CAPITALIZING ON CHANGE

Change offers many benefits to both organizations and individuals. But, the one thing it does not offer is to rewind the past. And, when you think you have finished the change cycle, it has only just begun. For the true benefit of change is that it is a part of our everyday lives and challenges us to keep moving forward with a focus on finding a better way and exploring opportunities. The alternative is to be left behind.

From personal growth to high performing teams, change brings to light fresh ideas, new leaders, and should ultimately deliver value to the shareholders. It can be motivating and exciting as well as disruptive. Change requires tenacity and persistence to endure the journey. t represents a false security of reaching the finish line. And, the beauty of change is that it is always waiting right around the corner. As we worked through the change wheels of the **hr**thought CHANGE Model, it became clear that in reality, change actually changes us. Simply put, change is a new way of doing things.

The benefits of change encourage individuals to be the change and move away from limited perceptions. These same individuals constitute formal and informal leaders that create the structure and culture to drive a growth trajectory and financial profitability in organizations. The success rate of change depends on high performance teams versus high performance individuals.

The success rate of the change process reflects how well the organization prepared for and managed through the change. The positive benefits of change include:

1) A more efficient operating model
2) Simplification of complex processes and policies
3) New leadership
4) Larger talent pool
5) New equipment
6) Better benefits and perks
7) Culture transformation
8) Re-energized workforce
9) New/clear vision

10) New technology
11) Automation of work processes
12) Achievable goals
13) New edge in the market
14) Acquired expertise in the industry
15) Cost savings from redundancies
16) New workspace
17) Ability to gain faster insights with data
18) Expanded Footprint
19) A stronger brand
20) Stronger market position

After the formal change process ends, there are still numerous details that still typically need to be wrapped up. These include: system feeds, automating work-around processes, final policy and procedure tweaks, internal website updates, company website changes, scheduled meetings with new leaders, follow up calls and evaluations, and continued questions from employees and customers.

COMMUNICATING THE FUTURE

It is essential to communicate updates to employees throughout the change cycle. Communication helps clarify where the company is in the change process and helps alleviate some of the anxiety when employees know what is going on.

Change can be exhausting for many people – senior leaders, managers, and individual employees. Taking the time to review the accomplishments to date, timeframes, challenges, schedule changes, and talk about what is to come prevents speculation and rumors. Given the need to keep employees focused, monthly updates work well. And, as significant milestones are reached, it is better to over-communicate successes and take advantage of the opportunity to recognize and reward achievements.

Most people like to be recognized for their contributions. Some of the most valued awards that I have used and seen other leaders use are plaques and framed certificates. Employees are proud to hang them in their cubicle or office. These types of recognition drive engagement and motivate employees to continue to work hard. I remember my son calling to tell me how excited he was that he was recognized by the CEO as the "Senior Software Engineer of the Year." There was no cash award or promotion attached—just a certificate—but he was so motivated by the recognition. As I have impressed upon many leaders over the years, it really is not all about money.

Companies use these opportunities to reinforce their values, commitment, and to celebrate small successes along the way. Celebrations can include a catered breakfast, pizza party, after-hours events, or even just a meeting to present awards. And, it is important to recognize employees at all levels of the organization and not just the same individuals who are perceived to "always win everything."

There are multiple ways to evaluate how well your communication strategy worked. For starters, employee engagement surveys are a great way to compile a short pulse survey and get feedback from your employees. The downside is that employees will give you their honest opinion about how things went, and the upside is that employees will give you their honest opinion. Lower scores are to be expected if you just completed a long change initiative. But, you can't change what you don't know.

Customer and vendor feedback are another source of valuable feedback. Sometimes they observe and hear things that do not get escalated to the senior leadership team. You can send out a formal survey or assign individuals to reach out by phone and capture this information.

WINNERS AND LOSERS

Vince Lombardi said that "Winners never quit, and quitters

never win." Given the roller coaster of change, there are bound to be people who are clearly winners as a result of their ability to work through change. And, there will be people who consider themselves a winner because they "never lose."

The individuals in the winner category were the ones who went above and beyond to deliver the desired outcome. They did not let things or people stand in their way, and they were probably one of the cheerleaders leading change. Winners are tenacious and persistent in achieving their goals. And, winners lead the way through their positive attitude, approach to change, flexibility, and willingness to go the distance.

As for the losers, it depends on how you define "loser." Everyone is a winner who is resilient and survives the organizational change. However, individuals who chose to leave the organization may be viewed as losers since they are missing the opportunity to move forward with the organization and reap the benefits of change. And, there will be individuals who are viewed as a loser because they were replaced or asked to take another role.

The idea of winners and losers, for the most part, is a perception on the part of others. Individuals must make personal choices to do what is right for them. And, for those who are impacted by change, as many people are, in today's workforce, they will have the opportunity to make different choices and pursue new opportunities. They may be considered a winner as well since there are often challenges for the employees remaining after a change event.

TALENT – POSITIONED TO WIN

Congratulations – you made it through the change. But, what did you learn about your internal talent pool? Did you have the internal expertise to assist with working through change? How did your leadership team perform? Did you identify new leaders through the change process? What are the skill gaps that need to be developed before the next change? And, were employees held accountable for their deliverables?

When companies review "lessons learned," they often forget to include a review of how their organization performed from a talent perspective. Talent is at a premium today, and it is becoming increasingly harder to find specific skill sets for some jobs. So, a post-change analysis is critical to:

(1) Identify skill gaps
(2) Review your succession plan
(3) Identify talent risks
(4) Evaluate the effectiveness of your recruiting process
(5) Validate your competencies
(6) Invest in your talent development programs
(7) Modify your performance management program
(8) Analyze attrition of employees

Succession plans cover executive and critical positions. But, what about other areas of the business where attrition may be an issue, or you face the loss of knowledge or pending retirements? This also requires a succession plan and talent strategy that goes further down in the organization.

The value of reviewing your internal talent structure after a change initiative is that you will have a fresh look at your talent pool after the impact of change given changes including new hires, replacements, and terminations (voluntary and involuntary). This review represents an opportunity to evaluate new and existing talent, establish a plan for personal growth of employees, and to focus on creating high performance teams versus high performing individuals.

As you review talent post-change, ask yourself some pointed questions:

- Was the organization able to adapt and change quickly?
- Is talent a competitive edge for you?

- In what areas are you strong from a leadership perspective?
- Where are you weak?
- What are your goals for the organization?
- Does the talent plan line up with the strategic goals?
- Are your managers prepared for the next change?

As a result of this review, you may also need to update your values, competencies, and succession plan for the organization. And, you may need to invest more in the areas of organization development and performance management.

CULTURE

Culture is who you say you are and how that expresses itself in your brand or product. Too often, I find that companies go through an expensive exercise of establishing visions and values, only to find that they are not living them internally. It is one thing to market your values on social media, your website, intranet, and promote to candidates. It is another thing to have those values internalized in your culture and for all employees to know and live them. Retention is typically the measure of whether or not you are who you say you are.

What is the best culture you have experienced? How do you recognize a great culture? A culture that is working is when you walk into a company and you can see and feel it. It is when employees are engaged and happy. It is when employees walk up to you and ask if they can help you. It is when employees are excited about what they are doing and proud of their company.

Applicants are interested in and ask about the company's values and vision. They research it and want to make sure that a company's culture is a good fit for them. As stated above, some companies go to great lengths to promote their culture and use it as a recruiting tool. They want to attract the best and the brightest and be known for having a cool and collaborative work environment. And, applicants are very interested in flexibility, career paths, and personal development.

A great discussion when you are about to go through change and when you complete the change cycle is, "Will our culture help us achieve our strategy?" What needs to change? What is the feedback from employees? Are we living our culture? Does the culture work for the future and help the company achieve its goals?

VALUES

As you think about values, the following is an example of 24 values found in organizations today. Keep in mind that values are shared beliefs. They represent a collaborative mindset for the entire team. The values listed below are in no particular order.

1. Integrity
2. Innovation
3. Creativity
4. Accountability
5. Boldness
6. Results
7. Respect
8. Customer Appreciation
9. Quality
10. Collaboration
11. Diversity
12. Teamwork
13. Speaking Up
14. Safety
15. Entrepreneurial ability
16. Leadership
17. Possibilities
18. Humbleness
19. Information
20. Constant Improvement
21. People
22. Empathy
23. Sustainability
24. Commitment

Once you go through a significant change, you may find that your old values do not fit your new world. It is important to communicate your values to all employees and to incorporate them into your hiring practices, performance management, and employee or professional development programs. Needless to say, values need to be lived from the top of the organization down and do not apply to just certain employees. Values are a great way to hold people accountable for their actions. Remember, that employees are watching senior leadership to see if the values apply to everyone. For example, if "Integrity" is a value of the company, then it goes against the culture to make exceptions and rehire individuals who were terminated for issues related to integrity.

Following are some areas to explore when evaluating your culture post-change:

1. Does your culture reward innovation?
2. Do you have a collaborative work environment?
3. Do you have a diverse workforce?
4. Do you have a diverse leadership team?
5. Are employees held accountable for their actions?
6. Are employees being developed?
7. How are decisions made?
8. How do employees handle conflict?

THE BENEFITS OF CHANGE FOR CUSTOMERS

A smooth transition and retention of customers is a top priority when going through change. Successfully managing change in this area means that you developed a communication strategy for the change initiatives to educate your customers on your pending change. As part of that process, you worked hard to minimize the effects of change for your customer base.

Staying connected to customers during a time of change and telling them what to expect has a strong correlation to customer retention. Your customers are probably going through changes in their organization, so they can relate to your challenges and perhaps learn from your experience. That said, this is a time when you need to make sure that your customer service is stellar and that your customers do not experience problems. While they understand, they do not understand when it impacts them.

Part of your evaluation of the benefits of change should include reviewing the following:

1. Did you have a comprehensive communication plan?
2. Were sales reps effectively trained on the change and how to communicate to the customers?
3. Did customers receive a written communication regarding the change?
4. Was there a website with contacts and Q&A for customers during the change?
5. What types of customer service issues were experienced during the change?
6. What were the breakdowns related to communication, if any?
7. What were the breakdowns related to customer service, if any?
8. What were the breakdowns related to systems, if any?
9. What were the breakdowns related to logistics, if any?
10. What customers did you lose during the change?
11. What challenges did you experience with the competition during the change?
12. What are the benefits to the customer as a result of the change?

Post-change is a great time to conduct a voice of the customer survey and get feedback directly from the customer. Customers do not like to complete lengthy questionnaires, but if you keep it simple and limit the number of questions, they are usually willing to provide valuable feedback.

The potential benefits to the customer include:

1. New Reporting
2. Faster Delivery Time
3. Simplification of the Ordering Process
4. Greater visibility to data – allowing them to make better decisions
5. New products
6. Automation of Manual Processes
7. Faster Response Time
8. Increased ROI
9. Alignment of Resources
10. New Services

As part of the customer review process, it is also a good time to have the sales reps circle back with the customer to review the benefits of change with them and to make sure they are taking advantage of the changes. You can offer educational workshops, understand any frustrations on their end, and make sure that they are benefiting from the recent change.

COMPETITIVE ANALYSIS

As part of the strategic planning process, executives typically conduct a Competitive Analysis to compare their company to the competition. This is often referred to as a SWOT (Strengths, Weaknesses, Opportunities, and Threats) Analysis. SWOT involves gathering information on the top competitors and comparing a number of factors to help determine if you have an effective strategy and where you need to focus your improvement efforts.

When conducting a SWOT analysis, some of the factors that are looked at are:

1. Market Segmentation
2. Revenue

3. Profitability
4. Size
5. Products/Services
6. Price
7. Edge/Differentiation
8. Marketing Strategy
9. Organization Structure
10. Strength of the Brand

Some of the resources that can be used to research information on the top competitors are:

1. Annual Reports
2. Trade Magazines
3. Trade Associations
4. Competition's Websites
5. Sales Force Assessment
6. Vendors
7. Customers
8. Dunn and Bradstreet
9. NYSE
10. Financial Websites

Prior to executing a new change, the SWOT should be reviewed to ensure everyone understands the gaps that need to be closed by the change initiative and the risks related to the competition. Competitors relish in using the perceived disruption of change to their advantage when calling on your customers. The conversation goes something like, "I know that Company X is going through a lot of change and struggling with their new system implementation, so I just wanted to reach out and see if I can help you."

As you conduct your review of what worked and did not work post-change, this is a critical area to review again. It is prudent to capture feedback from customers and sales reps to understand the competitions' tactics. You obviously had a game plan going into the change on how to handle the competition. Now, is the time to evaluate how well that plan worked and if you are in a better position to win against the competition.

- Did you take market share?
- Did you lose customers to the competition?
- Do you need to adjust your business plan?
- Did the competition create unexpected disruptions?
- As you look at the SWOT analysis, did you strengthen some of your weaknesses and offset some of the threats?
- What is your new edge – what differentiates your company in the market?

If you successfully kept the competition at bay during the change initiative, make sure you recognize the sales force for their contributions. If they were unable to fend off the competition, and you were faced with competitor disruptions and distractions, make sure you understand what happened and communicate the learning's to the sales force. Regardless of where you landed, it is important to analyze and communicate the results.

A big part of success is having more wins than losses. If that is the case, how will you use those wins to your advantage? How can you use your wins to market on social media, to the employee population, or in press releases? And, what "Intel" did you gain that will create more possibilities when contemplating future changes? The competitive analysis is a critical part of your post-change review process.

CASE STUDY 9
OVERWHELMED BY THE BENEFITS OF CHANGE

I worked for Company E in what I would call my first official executive leadership position. As soon as I arrived, Company E went through a large merger with a competitor. Strategically, the merger was brilliant and capitalized on gaining market share, a strong national account team, experienced senior leadership team, new product lines, a global footprint, and diversification of the workforce.

As I came to find out, the benefits of change in a merger can be so many that they actually become overwhelming for the organization to implement. Despite all the planning that went into the business transaction, it was a long haul for the organization and the "feet on the ground" to absorb and get their arms around. It was a challenge for everyone to keep pace with the change and to keep up with the barrage of emails and new processes and procedures that were released daily. Best practice manuals were published for every functional area, and it was impossible to keep up with all the conference calls and meetings.

The good news is that the senior leadership team heard the cry for help from the managers and worked to better prioritize the key initiatives and to respect the fact that the field was not sitting at their computers waiting for emails and more directives from corporate. One of the key lessons learned by the corporate office was that they had to make change more manageable and that they could not have all functional areas dictating multiple changes at the same time.

Through collaboration and assistance provided to the managers, all of the changes were successfully implemented over a two-year period of time. When completed, the divisions were in a much stronger position to compete in the market based on faster systems, a new CRM, stronger leadership, and a focus on talent development.

As companies explore change, it is important to not only plan the change but to be cognizant of, and avoid where possible, conflicting initiatives that stretch your resources too thin. Companies can set themselves and their employees up for failure by not recognizing potential burnout and the fact that pushing too many things at once leads to sacrificing quality. The benefits of change are many, and key to successfully managing through change is communication, planning, resources, and execution.

POST-CHANGE EFFECTIVENESS SUMMARY

This summary is intended to provide a consolidated look by functional area and overall company view of the end results of a change initiative. You could also use a red, yellow, and green color code to represent the wins (green), losses (red), or >80% (yellow). This format offers one example of how information can be communicated to the appropriate individuals in the organization and used as a performance tool.

Function	Goal	Results	% Goal Achieved	Comments
Sales	+5% Sales Growth	4% Growth	80%	
Sales	+2% Margin Improvement	2% Margin Improvement	100%	On Target.
Finance	Reduce Overhead by 10%	9.5% Reduction	95%	Addt'l. 5% will come from headcount.
Finance	Budget for Change Initiative - $300,000	$320,000	+7% Over Budget	Overage to come out of Operations.
Marketing	New SVP Marketing	Hired	100%	
Marketing	New CRM	Implemented	100%	Completed within Scheduled Timeframe. All users trained.
HR	Outsourced Payroll	Outsourced	100%	All employees paid correctly in first cycle.
Communications	New Website	Off Schedule	85%	Two-week Delay with Vendor.
Operations	New Logistics Tracking	Complete	100%	Smooth Transition with 100% Compliance.
IT	New Reporting Tool for External Customers	Behind Schedule one week	90%	Unexpected error in Summary Module.
Executive	Communication to All Employees	On Schedule	100%	Conference Calls and Emails.

Capturing "Lessons Learned" immediately after implementing a change initiative is important while it is fresh in everyone's mind. These lessons capture gaps by functional area and also reveal themes/gaps across the organization. This can be a useful guide for developing skill gaps and in planning future projects or change initiatives.

LESSONS LEARNED

Function	Worked	Did Not Work	Learning
Operations		Expense Reduction	Needed to review weekly with managers.
Operations	Implementation of New Logistics Tracking Tool	Challenged to get all Drivers Trained	Build in more time for training and Follow up.
IT	Faster Reporting Tool for Customers	Unexpected error	Timing too compressed and did not allow for unexpected problems.
Sales	Marginal Improvement through bundled products	Achieving sales growth	Target too aggressive.
Communications	Initial Communication to Employees	Needed more updates along the way	Build in weekly updates.

COACHING QUESTIONS - Chapter 7

Below are some suggested Coaching Questions you may want to consider for a post-change review process:

1. What was missed in delivering the desired outcome?
2. What were the gaps, if any, in the communication plan?
3. How did the disruption impact the business?
4. How did the company perform against the targeted goals?
5. What was the impact on key talent? Attrition overall?
6. What customers were lost/gained as a result of the change?
7. How did customers benefit from the change?
8. How did the organization perform against the budget for change?
9. What areas of focus need to be addressed after the change?
10. What were the lessons learned?
11. What are the strengths of the organization after the change?
12. What are the weaknesses of the organization after the change?
13. How will you prepare leaders for the future?
14. What stood out from an organizational development perspective?
15. What efficiencies were gained from a systems perspective?
16. What, if anything failed from an execution perspective?
17. Did you increase market share?
18. Do you need to adjust your business plan?
19. Did the competition create unexpected disruptions?
20. As you look at the SWOT analysis, did you strengthen some of your weaknesses and offset some of the threats?
21. What is your new edge, and what differentiates your company in the market?

CHAPTER 8

CONCLUSION
NOW IT'S YOUR TURN

Be the change that you wish to see in the world.
~ Mahatma Gandhi

REVIEW OF The hrthought CHANGE Model

Be the Change identifies the six (6) events that occur during change in an organization. The **hr**thought CHANGE Model then aligns the people impact and processes with each event. This model goes way beyond change management and establishes a change framework to help leaders embrace change with confidence and to increase the success rate of their change initiatives.

The **hr**thought CHANGE Model is scalable, easy to follow, and provides a structured approach, complete with case studies and coaching questions to help evaluate your specific needs. Each event is represented as a change wheel in the model. The model is designed to take into consideration the whole individual while creating awareness and acceptance around common change dynamics.

Following is a high-level review of the six (6) change events in the model. Return to the various Chapters based on these change events, and areas where you need increased focus, routinely.

CHANGE WHEEL #1 – FEAR OF CHANGE

As highlighted at the beginning of the book, "Change is the #1 fear in the heart of executives today." Given the pace of change, disruption of technology, and the high failure rate of change initiatives, change requires change-leaders and a better strategy for tomorrow.

The fear of change wheel encourages you to "lean into the change and turn right." By making that turn, as a leader, you can be the change that guides your organization with a vision and purpose while keeping a constant eye on the implications to employees. It reinforces the importance of a strong leadership team working collaboratively with the CEO to evaluate and drive the change.

Change is a major undertaking that requires upfront due diligence, a clear strategy and plan, and training and communication alignment to succeed. Change impacts employees and customers and can present risks to your strategic plan and financial targets.

The fear of change wheel highlights the competencies for executives leading through change and also speaks to the importance of leaders capitalizing on executive presence, style, and influence during change events. It is thought-provoking, walks you through the initial fears and risks, and helps you prepare for the disruption to come.

CHANGE WHEEL #2 – DISRUPTION

Change challenges the status quo and brings with it varying degrees of disruption. Studies estimate the failure rate of organizational initiatives to be anywhere from 60-70%. And, sadly enough, approximately 53% of employees report no leadership development opportunities in their organization.

The change wheel of disruption explores the difference of being a disruptive leader versus being a leader managing change through disruption. It also reviews the watch-outs and distractions of change, including distrust, stress, and politics.

Disruption impacts the business and employees. It is famous for creating chaos and confusion and causes some employees to go into survival mode. This change wheel will help you anticipate disruptions from the competition, think about the end game, and offers valuable insights into the importance of communication.

CHANGE WHEEL #3 – COMMUNICATION

The communication change wheel defines how you talk about change to the organization. It highly recommends that you speak so the organization listens to your message. It highlights the power and influence of communication and the importance of PACC (Purpose, Audience, Clear, and Concise) when communicating.

Platforms of communication are reviewed along with tips to consider when planning and executing a communication plan. A sample communication template is also included to guide you through the planning process.

The communication change wheel offers approaches to minimize distrust and stresses the importance of informal leaders. There is also a section on communicating with customers and watch-outs about the competition. And, some thoughts are included regarding being prepared for the media and the impact of social media in today's work environment.

CHANGE WHEEL #4 – NAVIGATION

The navigation change wheel helps you maneuver the change journey by ensuring that change is being led from the top of the organization. It introduces LIL (Lead, Inspire, and Listen) as a way to guide the vision of change but hold individuals accountable during change.

Certainly of interest, is the defined role of the manager and the coach in this chapter. There is also guidance around the growing importance of team effectiveness in organizations and tips for making change easier for employees.

The final section of navigation talks about connecting employees to the change instead of allowing them to struggle through change as an individual. It also speaks to the benefits of empowerment and inspiring employees to be "ambassadors of change." Navigation is not only about where change is headed but questions what is working and not working at this point in change.

CHANGE WHEEL #5 – REINVENTION

Reinvention is where the future state of the organization meets the final alignment of the steps to get there. It signals that it is time to leave the disruption behind and fully integrate the elements of the change strategy.

The reinvention change wheel recognizes the importance of an open mindset and embracing new opportunities as the organization implements change. It addresses resistance and the needs of employees beyond today.

There are several trends identified with powerful discussion points. They are:
1. Tomorrow's Leaders
2. The Impact of More Female Leaders in the Work Environment
3. The Work Environment of the Future

This is probably my favorite event of change, and the one that has the biggest impact moving forward. I also included an article I published, "The Courage to Excel as a Female." Reinvention wraps up by looking at the impact on employees when they move from fear of change to the reality of change. It concludes with several great case studies and some powerful coaching questions.

CHANGE WHEEL #6 – BENEFITS OF CHANGE

The Benefits of Change wheel starts with capturing the process of measuring the effectiveness of change. It walks through a qualitative and quantitative analysis for stakeholders. And, it strongly recommends reviewing and documenting lessons learned as a way to benefit from success and learn from failure.

Equally important, this chapter covers steps for communicating feedback to employees and soliciting their feedback through an engagement survey. And, it shares thoughts around "winners and losers" that are often debated during change.

This chapter includes a list of potential benefits of change. It takes a look at conducting a post-change review of talent, culture, and the benefits of change for customers.

As part of the post-change effective analysis, a competitive analysis is recommended. This analysis reveals your wins in this area, unexpected disruptions, and how you can use your gains to your advantage.

The Benefits of Change also includes sample templates for preparing a Post-Change Effectiveness Summary and capturing Lessons Learned.

How You Can Use The hrthought CHANGE Model In Your Organization

Be The Change is designed to help you grow your business by leveraging change through the benefit of your leaders and their teams. This means developing and investing in your leaders and building high performance teams. One of the keys to capitalizing on change is to maximize the effectiveness of your teams.

Teams are a critical part of organizations in the future and play a major role in determining if your change initiatives succeed or fail. And, it is time that leaders direct their efforts to develop high performance teams versus maintaining a more narrow focus on high performers. The power of the team is far greater than continuing to focus on a few high potentials in organizations.

If you are a leader contemplating change in your organization, the **hr**thought CHANGE Model can assist you with identifying common failure points, preparing your managers for change, and creating a roadmap for your company to be more agile in managing through change. You can become a catalyst for change and navigate the landmines of change while you measure the effectiveness of change and invest in your leadership team.

Be The Change is a guide for experienced and new leaders who want to take an inclusive approach to change. You can benefit from leveraging real-life case studies and lessons learned throughout the book. It provides a structure to assist you with working through all six (6) events of change or focusing on one area where you are struggling or need more help.

Starting with the Fear of Change, you will gain insight into anticipating the impact on the business, executives, managers, individuals, and generational differences. You will be better prepared to understand the true impact of fear and anxiety as it relates to change. And, you can take advantage of the model to evaluate the purpose of change and develop a comprehensive change strategy.

There are multiple checklists and templates in the book to help you get started and aligned with your specific change initiatives. These tools give you a platform from which to build your customized solutions.

Checklists and tools include:
1. Project Plan for Change
2. Due Diligence Checklist

3. Coaching Questions at the end of each Chapter relative to change events
4. Case Studies
5. Defining Platforms for Communication
6. Communication Plan
7. Sample Values for Organizations
8. Post-Change Checklist
9. Evaluating Benefits for Customers
10. Competitive Analysis
11. Post-Change Effectiveness Summary
12. Lessons Learned

The **hr**thought CHANGE Model is your guide to leading change with confidence. It is thought-provoking, will help you anticipate distractions, and will create a focus on discipline and accountability to achieve your goals. Leaders will be prepared to take on the challenge of managing through change, and employees can become ambassadors for change. And, one of the biggest benefits of the model is that it allows you to actualize change in incremental steps.

Be The Change is a great tool to use to educate your leadership team around change and to help generate a change management strategy. It can be used to supplement change management training as well as help your leaders align organization needs across the events of the **hr**thought CHANGE framework.

Prioritizing your time as a leader and investing in the right people and types of change will make it easier to embrace the constant demands of change in the work environment today and in the future. You will be able to see the possibilities of change versus the disruption of change. And, you will learn to effectively align the people side of the equation with the key change events and process foundation. The emphasis should be on spending less time on creating templates and more time focused on the people impact for each change event.

For additional assistance with creating a change strategy or using the **hr**thought CHANGE Model to work through change in your organization, email us at: **info@hrthought.com** or visit our website at: **www.hrthought.com** to request more information.

COACHING FOR THE FUTURE

There is a misconception today that coaching is easy. And so, it seems that there are an overwhelming number of people taking up coaching as a profession. For many coaches, their definition of coaching is "telling people what to do."

I believe that the coach of the future will need to be more business savvy, more attuned to social and cultural needs and demands, and be experienced in working through change and the reinvention of companies and individuals. This will require many coaches to be certified and competent in coaching tomorrow's leaders through the pace of change, while balancing employee/talent needs.

At the forefront of opportunities for leaders and coaches are diversity and inclusion, the push for more females in leadership positions, equality for females, a totally different work environment, and ever-changing advancements in technology. So, as you search for a coach in the future, search for someone who can "meet you on your level" and be a trusted confidante.

COACHING QUESTIONS - Chapter 8

Below are some suggested Coaching Questions to consider when working through your "Change" Strategy:

1. How can you use the **hr**thought CHANGE Model in your organization?
2. What change wheels provide the biggest insight?
3. What will you do differently?
4. How will this change model help you train your managers?
5. What is the most valuable part of the change model?
6. What tools/checklists can you implement?
7. How does this change the way you have been managing change?
8. How will you place emphasis on the people side of the equation?

APPENDIX A

PROJECT PLAN TEMPLATES

Following are examples of project plan templates you could use to document the goals and metrics for your change initiatives:

I. Corporate Project Plan
Restructuring/Reduce Costs by $40M

Goal	Metrics	Owner	Date/ Deliverable	Status
Review Operations Expenses	Reduce overhead by $40M	CEO/CFO	TBD	

The above project plan reflects the overall goal of reducing overhead costs by $40M for the company. Then, each functional area would have a project plan (following page) detailing how the expenses would be reduced in their area.

NOTES
_____
_____
_____
_____
_____
_____

II. Operations Project Plan
Restructuring/Reduce Costs by $40M

Goal	Metrics	Owner	Date/ Deliverable	Status
Close 20 Facilities	Reduce overhead by $20M	SVP Ops	TBD	Achieved
Eliminate (10) Regional Manager positions	Reduce payroll costs by $10M	SVP Ops/ Director Ops	TBD	Achieved
Automate Inventory Processes	Achieve efficiency savings of $10M			Achieved $7M savings – fell short $3M

NOTES

APPENDIX B

DUE DILIGENCE ACTIVITIES

When you are evaluating an acquisition or an investment, a great starting point for performing due diligence activities is as follows. Due diligence is a process of verification and auditing to analyze financials, key processes, and compliance related to an investment, in order to make informed decisions.

1. **Antitrust and Regulatory Issues** – Federal and state laws that may impact the formation and operation of a business.
2. **Assets – Buildings/Land/Equipment/Other** – List of all assets owned or leased by a business.
3. **Employment Agreements** – Understanding all obligations and the terms of employment agreements for senior leaders and other employees.
4. **Employee Relations Actions** – Review of current and past employee performance actions, patterns, and the corrective action process.
5. **Environmental Issues** – Understanding any environmental problems that pose a risk or existing issues.
6. **Evaluation of Governance Practices** – Audit compliance with mandated government legislation.
7. **Evaluation of Systems and Security** – Evaluate systems, integration opportunities, security practices, and cyber security.
8. **E-Verify Process and Compliance** – Verification of E-Verify compliance.
9. **Expected synergies from the acquisition** – Evaluation and analysis of anticipated efficiencies, financial synergies, products, customers, talent, and footprint.

10. **Facilities/Redundant Locations/Potential Closures** – Evaluation of footprint to understand where there are redundancies, capacity issues, and potential facility closures.
11. **Financial Impact of the acquisition** – Financial gains and improvements as a result of a merger, acquisition, or investment.
12. **Financial Statement Analysis** – Analyzing a company's financial statements to understand the overall well-being of the company in order to make financial decisions.
13. **Impact on Employees** – Evaluate redundancy of talent, benefits, location changes, skills, compensation, and other employee related items.
14. **Insurance Policies** – Legal review of all applicable insurance policies and risks.
15. **Leadership/Talent Pool** – Review succession planning, hi-potentials, and talent pool.
16. **Leases** – Legal review of all leases, contracts, obligations, and term clauses.
17. **Liabilities** – Review liabilities to ensure that vendors, banks, suppliers, etc. are being repaid according to the terms of the agreements.
18. **Material Contract Reviews** – Legal review of all material contracts.
19. **Pending Lawsuits/Litigation** – Complete list and review of all pending lawsuits and litigation activities, as well as recent activity.
20. **Pivotal Investments Required** – Investments required to fund an investment and make it work.
21. **Safety Metrics** – Understand current safety metrics as compared to the industry, and review best practices and processes in place.
22. **Subcontractors** – Review of all authorized subcontractors, agreements, and term clauses.
23. **Technology/Intellectual Property** – Audit the value of the technology and the number and quality of the intellectual property.
24. **Worker's Compensation Claims** – Review and evaluate all current claims, trends, recent activity over the past few years, and review processes in place.

APPENDIX C

SUMMARY OF COACHING QUESTIONS

Chapter 1 – Introduction of hrthought Change Model

1. What is the full scope of the change?
2. What are the possibilities and ideas behind the pending change?
3. How can I prepare my team for change?
4. Who will lead the change initiative?
5. What does the end state look like?
6. Who will be impacted by the change?
7. What external resources do I need to engage?
8. What am I missing?

Chapter 2 – Fear of Change

1. Who do you need to engage first?
2. How prepared is your team to manage change?
3. What are the skill gaps?
4. Which team members need to be involved immediately?
5. What concerns will the Board of Directors raise?
6. Who can you trust?
7. How much information do you need to share and how deep in the organization?
8. How will the change impact your financial targets for the year?
9. What are the trade-offs?
10. Who can lead the change effort?
11. Do you need a PMO (project management office)?
12. Who will head the PMO?

13. What does an ideal project plan look like to manage the change?
14. What are the key milestones that need to be addressed?
15. How and when will you communicate the change?
16. How do you address fears and rumors?
17. Who will the change impact from an organizational standpoint?
18. What are your options?
19. What are the risks?
20. How will the change impact your customers?
21. How will you handle the competition?
22. What can go wrong?
23. Who are the hi-potential talent risks?
24. Will you need retention bonuses?

Chapter 3 – Disruption

1. What is the purpose behind the disruption?
2. What are the risks?
3. What can be done to minimize the disruption to the employees and the business?
4. What competitor is our biggest threat?
5. How does disruption help us move ahead of the competition?
6. How will the competition react?
7. What does disruption mean to our customers?
8. What is the expected timeframe for the disruption?
9. Are we at risk of losing key talent?
10. What are we missing?
11. What is the message to the sales force?
12. What tools do we need for the sales force?
13. What politics are being played in the organization?
14. What is the "End Game?"

Chapter 4 – Communication

1. What is the purpose of the communication?
2. What are we communicating?
3. How much should we communicate?

4. What medium should we use to communicate the change?
5. When should we communicate the change?
6. What is the timeline for the change?
7. Who should be involved in laying out the Communication Plan?
8. Who is the primary person to lead the Communication Plan?
9. Who is the audience?
10. What internal resources do we have?
11. What external resources do we need?
12. What best practices do we have to rely on from previous change announcements?
13. How do we communicate to and train the managers?
14. Do we need FAQ's (Frequently Asked Questions)?

Chapter 5 – Navigation

1. How can we successfully navigate this change?
2. What skills do I need to develop?
3. What skills are missing on the leadership team?
4. What resources does the team need?
5. How do I create a safe environment?
6. How do I connect employees to a common cause?
7. When will they let go of the past?
8. What am I missing?
9. Where should my time be spent?
10. How do I address unproductive behaviors?
11. How are the employees feeling about the change?
12. How do I make the change easier for employees?
13. How can I more effectively communicate updates?
14. What is working?
15. What is not working?

Chapter 6 – Reinvention

1. How do I create a "reinvention" mindset?
2. What are the gaps in the talent strategy?
3. How do we develop employees for the future?
4. What competencies do we need for leaders in the future?

5. How can my team benefit from coaching?
6. What challenges do we face as we roll out the new business model?
7. How do we create a coaching culture?
8. What is changing about our work environment?
9. What is the impact of technology on employees?
10. How do I communicate the changes to our customers?
11. How do I leverage generational differences?
12. What knowledge do I need to protect?
13. What policies need to be replaced?
14. What is the plan to support the new roles in the organization?
15. What is the impact of more female leaders in the organization?
16. What is our diversity and inclusion strategy?

Chapter 7 – Benefits of Change

1. What was missed in delivering the desired outcome?
2. What were the gaps, if any, in the communication plan?
3. How did the disruption impact the business?
4. How did the company perform against the targeted goals?
5. What was the impact on key talent? Attrition overall?
6. What customers were lost/gained as a result of the change?
7. How did customers benefit from the change?
8. How did the organization perform against the budget for change?
9. What areas of focus need to be addressed after the change?
10. What were the lessons learned?
11. What are the strengths of the organization after the change?
12. What are the weaknesses of the organization after the change?
13. How will you prepare leaders for the future?
14. What stood out from an organizational development perspective?
15. What efficiencies were gained from a systems perspective?
16. What, if anything, failed from an execution perspective?
17. Did you increase market share?
18. Do you need to adjust your business plan?
19. Did the competition create unexpected disruptions?

20. As you look at the SWOT analysis, did you strengthen some of your weaknesses and offset some of the threats?
21. What is your new edge, and what differentiates your company in the market?

Chapter 8 – Conclusion

1. How can you use the **hr**thought Change model in your organization?
2. What change wheels provide the biggest insight?
3. What will you do differently?
4. How will this change model help you train your managers?
5. What is the most valuable part of the change model?
6. What tools/checklists can you implement?
7. How does this change the way you have been managing change?
8. How will you place an emphasis on the people side of the equation?

REFERENCES

Andrews J., Cameron H., and Harris M. (2008). Journal of Organizational Change Management.
https://www.emeraldinsight.com/doi/abs/10.1108/09534810810874796

Ashkenas, Ron. (2013). Change Management Needs to Change.
https://hbr.org/2013/04/change-management-needs-to-cha.html

Catalyst (2017). Women on Corporate Boards Globally.
https://www.catalyst.org/knowledge/women-corporate-boards-globally

DeSilver, Drew. (2018). Women scarce at top of U.S. business – and in the jobs that Lead there.
http://www.pewresearchorg/author/ddesilver/

Denning, Steve. (2016). What You Need To Know About Disruption: John Hagel.
https://www.forbes.com/sites/stevedenning/2016/02/29/john-hagel-fresh-research-on-disruption/#41e21a0d236e

Fast Company (2018). The World's 50 Most Innovative Companies 2018.
https://www.fastcompany.com/most-innovative-companies/2018

Garvey, Hugh. (2018). How Netflix CEO Reed Hastings Built a $170 Billion Entertainment Empire.
>https://www.maxim.com/entertainment/reed-hastings-netflix-ceo-profile- 2018-8

Global Workplace Analytics.com (2018). Latest Telecommuting Statistics.
>https://globalworkplaceanalytics.com/telecommuting-statistics

Ibarra, Herminia, Ely, Robin J., and Kolb, Deborah M. (2013). Women Rising: The Unseen Barriers.
>https://hbr.org/2013/09/women-rising-the-unseen-barriers

Lavoie, Andre. (2017). Is Your Employee Development Broken? Here's How to Fix It.
>https://www.entrepreneur.com/article/288578

Nohria, Nitin, and Beer, Michael. (2000). Cracking the Code of Change.
>https://hbr.org/2000/05/cracking-the-code-of-change

Pew Research Center. What Makes a Good Leader, and Does Gender Matter?
>http://www.pewsocialtrends.org/2015/01/14/chapter-2-what-makes-a-good-leader-and-does-gender-matter

Society of Human Resource Management. (2017). Executive Summary – Employee Job Satisfaction and Engagement.
>https://www.shrm.org/hr-today/trends-and-forecasting/research-and-surveys/Documents/2017-Employee-Job-Satisfaction-and-Engagement-Executive-Summary.pdf

The Economist. (September 2018). Silicon Valley – A victim of its own success.

Turner, Dawn-Marie. (2009). Navigating the White Space of Change.
    http://www.refresher.com/admtwhite.html

About Robin

Robin Reininger is the Founder and CEO of **hr**thought, LLC. She is a former Fortune 500 Executive who leverages a prolific background with intuitive problem-solving skills and pragmatic forward thinking.

Ms. Reininger founded **hr**thought, LLC to help companies grow their business by leveraging change through the benefit of their leaders and their teams. She places a high emphasis on developing leaders and high performance teams to increase the success rate of key initiatives. The professional services available from **hr**thought, LLC include: *Leadership Coaching, HR Strategy, and Educational Workshops.*

Prior to founding **hr**thought, Ms. Reininger held Executive positions in Human Resources and Sales with: Velcro Companies, TopBuild Corporation, Masco Contractor Services, Avery Dennison, Staples, and Corporate Express. Robin's accomplishments include:

1) Being a member of a team that took a company public.
2) Taking a direct sales model from $40M to a $300M national inside sales model.
3) Rolling out a global consultative sales model that improved profitability.

Robin Reininger has an MBA from DeSales University and a BA in Business Administration from Washington and Jefferson College. She is certified as an Executive Coach through the Center for Executive Coaching. In addition, her credentials include: SPHR, MBTI, ESCI, and Certifications in Human Capital, Transformational Leadership, and Strategic Selling.

Visit: www.hrthought.com for more detailed information on the professional services.

CPSIA information can be obtained
at www.ICGtesting.com
Printed in the USA
BVHW040006180419
545790BV00007B/312/P

Strategy
Project Plan
    Milestones
    Measures of Success
            Ex- ↓ loss, baseline lost

- Soca Leader to mg Δ
  Preparedness to own Δ
- Success Plan + Reduction Bias?

melien
→ people pu
→ prove
→ rider
→ laws